When Life Goes Crumbling

When Life

Goes Crumbling

Published in New York, NY

Names and places are the product of the author's imagination and are used fictitiously. Any resemblance to actual persons, living or dead, or locales is entirely coincidental.

The views expressed are those of the author and do not reflect the views or position of the United States Army, Department of Defense, or United States Government.

ISBN: 978-0-578-90548-8

Library of Congress Control Number: 2021909306

First Paperback edition 2021

Table of Contents

“Arriving on a nightmare, praying for a dream”

-Maya Angelou

Prologue

College. I had arrived on a nightmare and prayed on a dream as Maya Angelou would say in her poem "On the Pulse of the Morning". Oftentimes, I found myself questioning, is it worth it? I once stepped foot on campus with the hopes of becoming an Army Officer with a first-class ticket to middle class, and a degree at what they would call "The premier leadership development institute" who also happened to be the number one public school in the nation at the time. But as I embarked on this journey, I faced more and more challenges that I had not planned on encountering. It was at this very institution where I found myself for the first time mentally-defeated, medically declining, and peacefully broken, all the while of being surrounded by people who didn't understand me or were self-absorbed. It was in these times where I found myself constantly saying, is it worth it? Is my sanity, peace, happiness, and dignity worth a direct flight to middle-class? I spent all my years there praying on a dream that wasn't promising. I then began to question, am I willing to put my life on the line for a country who would not do the same for me? It was at this moment I realized that I am putting myself on the line for a country that will do nothing for me, but pay me middle-class money with the risk of my entire existence. I slowly noticed that my dreams were disguised as nightmares. It was like I saw the "no poverty" sign and ignored the "no peace" sign then purchased "Army Officer" at a cost of life. So, is it worth it?

Through all of this, I convinced myself to wait for a dream that fought hard against me because I did not want to quit. In this process, I developed raging anxiety that slowly turned into raging depression. Even though I conquered every obstacle, my mind had gotten weaker and weaker. It was in these low moments where I used poetry as a place to vent and hide my feelings at the same time. Little did I know, it would be my poetry that put on a cape and swooped in to save my life. But, all these low moments trapped my thoughts, and I found myself stuck in a dark grey campus full of people who just merely did not understand. Poetry was a place where I expressed my pain, my hurt, and my intellect. Even though poetry seemed to have been my saving grace, it also served as my poison. In the times I was ready to exit this world with a mind who felt purposeless, I used poetry as a place to not cause a ruckus. My poetry both silenced and heightened my voice. But I'm here today to show you the dark side of the moon, and unexplored wonders of the world. We constantly ask ourselves what is life, but not often do we ask how to conquer it. I asked myself this every single day oftentimes wondering why I am facing all of these obstacles or why when I finally overcome them, everything comes crashing and burning. These are things that I cannot seem to understand. I am going to tell you my story, however, beware because the details are disheartening, horrific, and emotionally driven. This is not for the weak minded, or people who struggle with controlling their own emotions. For this purpose, I do not recommend it. Here is my story of when life goes crumbling.

Phase 1:

The Build Up

Ch 1: Anxiety

Anxiety is when your heart wants so much more and your mind says "Bitch you trippin'". A sense of inner turmoil leaks throughout my body as my experiences that define life come to haunt me. This feeling of nervousness and doubt is one that attacks the mind, so much so, that physical symptoms begin to appear. The lack of control and uncertainty causes so much stress that your mind produces unanswerable questions that causes your spirit to ache. Characterized by worry and restlessness, it too came to haunt me.

Concluding the deaths of close friends and health issues filled with uncertainty, I spent every day fearful of what was next to come. This was only the beginning of a build-up that I had not planned on facing any time soon. And to make things worse, the more life experiences I had faced, the more I had to be apprehensive about.

To be silenced is to be denied the opportunity to speak your truth. To be alone is to have no one to confide in to uplift your spirit. I was in a place in life where I believed that there was no such thing as someone helping you because, quite frankly, I did not believe anyone would understand. But a wise one once said lean not on your own understanding, and I did just that. You only cry for help if you believe there's help to cry for. I lived in a position where on the east side of the river is what held all the fulfilling things in life, but I had resided on the west where there was nothing but your intellectual being.

I was in a place where geese go to poop because that was all it was good for. I was in a place where rivers freeze so boats can't pass by. I was in a place where gray is the stone of choice and storms come to vent. I was in a place of silent screams and barred windows. I was in a place where suspicions are quickly silenced and the out-spoken get the boot. I was in a place where the outsiders admire, and the insiders despise. I was at the worst point.

This is a place where the broken break more, depression is silenced, and help is for the weak. This is a place where the only help you get is to be told to be resilient. This is a place where prescriptions mask pain, and the pain builds mountains. This is a place where respect is given from the bottom up and never the top down. This is a place where comparisons are the popular poison of choice. This is a place where we wear the mask and trying to look perfect exists. Welcome to the worst point in the west.

This is a place where the fear of your worst nightmares becoming reality haunt you. I was in a position where malicious intent is always hidden behind the curtains, and where your beliefs must be in line with the system or else you are not fit for it. God forbid you fail one or two times, then the fear alone will make you its first victim. It is a place where you are used as a symbol of deterrence. There is no room for even the thought of imperfection at the worst point in the west. This is a place where depression and suicidal thoughts are only one phone call away, but the fear of it all sends you into a frenzy. This is a place where you can expect the worst and get just that. A place where the lower echelons are inferior, and the present is equal to the past. A place where trust is broadcasted but not practiced. This place is called Anxiety.

This sense of inner turmoil is what weakened my mind and prepared me to be prey for what was to come next. It was something that haunted me every single morning at the worst point in the west. The only way that I knew how to deal with this feeling or at least ease it was to write poetry and conceptualize what is affecting me. When I feel nothing else will work, I can always count on poetry to assist me in my journey. Little did I know, when I had written Anxiety, I was attempting to write it out of my life.

Anxiety

I wake up every morning and I question my life
I go to sleep every night and I pray I get right
The tensions getting thick, I can cut it with a knife
I question my existence every day like

Do I really want the fame?
Do I really want the light?
Can I really take the pain?
Can I really win the fight?

How I deal with all this pain, I always ask myself
And if God had turned his back, should I blast myself?
If no one knows about the struggle, how do I ask for help
Cuz these pills don't ever work, it just masks myself

I'm sick of all this drama and this pain and hurt
Because I am tryna figure out what all this pain is worth
But my mind is always dead because it's chained and burnt
And my thoughts go insane when I feel this pain on earth

Day by day I wonder if I'm ever going to make it
My life is like a gamble and I think I might take it
My mind is about to blow, and my thoughts are really shaken
I caked up all my pills and I know I'm not gon' make it

Can I ever be saved if this death is always teasing
Yelling, "Can you Call a doctor! The Preacher! The deacon!"
Cuz when I always call, it seems like God is always sleeping
And if this God ain't never here, I'll call the devil for a meeting

Oh my god, I'm about to panic

The pressure's going up
My mind is acting frantic
And my heart is beating rough
This is tough
This is enough
Both my hands are in a cuff
How do I rise from all this pain,
if my rise is not enough?
How come these lies are not contained
and my cries don't call their bluff
How come this life is not to blame
when this life is one that's crushed
How can I abstain from all these chains
if my brain is in a rush
My pain is plain in some champagne
that I drink until its hush
The anxiety is killing me
And it's taking my soul
But if anxiety takes life
Them my life would be sold

Cold
Is how I feel when the devils in my presence
It's like he gave me a bottle and at the bottom there's a message
A cheat sheet is in the message with a list full of lessons
But I had to drink what was in it to get to all those lessons

I can tell them I'm fine, but I know I'm not ok
You can call it murder but I will call it grace
I got nowhere to live, that's why I can't stay
And if I go tomorrow, I don't care what'd they say

I got no one to talk to because they lost too
Someone said, “I’ll kill myself,” and I said “true”
They popped pills and slit wrists but that’s nothing new
Many people said they can help but I said “who?”

I'm fading away
I’m drinking my problems away
I know I ain't perfect but I try every day
If peace is the product, then what’s the price to pay

I don’t want to go back and think of those times
Think of those times when I took all them pills
When it took four tries and I still didn’t heal
I’m not paying the price now, but just send me the bill

Anxiety

Ch 2: Manhattan

Living in Manhattan is pretty expensive but drowning in it is even more costly. Manhattan was my pain disguised as pleasure. It was an alcoholic beverage used to serve the purpose of getting my mind off things and having a good time despite disheartening circumstances. I was oblivious to the dark path I was traveling upon. I wanted to live a normal life with my abnormal circumstances, so I normalized a "Manhattan" as a representation of drinking away my chaos in a form of pleasure. I drank so much that I banked on drinking one too many to forget the memories of displeasure. I thought a blackout or two will do the trick, but in this sense, Manhattan would serve as my poison. When that day came when I badly wanted nothing but to remember, I was afraid of what I would. I had not known what had happened to me the night before, but I was left with the feelings of the morning after. It was at this moment when I felt like falling from tall buildings in Manhattan. I knew what I had felt, and that feeling described every detail of what happened the night before without me knowing what actually happened. That "one too many" has haunted me every day. I tried so hard to forget a memory or two when drinking a Manhattan, but on that day, it left a lasting one.

The high life of Manhattan caused me to become vulnerable to my surroundings. It redefined what I called home. After that night, Manhattan became so bad in my mind that every breath I breathed was a dosage of poison. I guess the city that never slept finally caught up to me. I characterized it as the devil's drink of choice. The drink I described as the city of dreams had ruined my life because it provided nothing but the sweet taste of defeat.

That night I went broke; so broke that I couldn't afford happiness, peace, and my rent to keep my home. It all fell apart when Manhattan left me a lasting memory worth dying for. It was the night when Manhattan finally cost too much, and all I remembered was the sweet taste of Manhattan. A lot of people say the real you comes out when your inhibitions are lowered. But sometimes the real you is defined by what you won't do when they aren't. But knowing who I am and using poetry as my therapy, I used my pen to pay the price and wrote "Manhattan."

Manhattan

You Low-Down Dirty Bastard!
You ruined my life!!
City of dreams my ass
Even though you were my drink of choice
Oh, how I loved the sweet taste of Manhattan

It was like large buildings falling down my throat
As taxi's travelled down my taste buds during rush hour
Pollution browning up my liver
As the taste of Manhattan settles on my tongue
Sighs Manhattan.

The city of dreams giving me optical illusions with every sip
Walking with a dance in every step as I cross the street in times square
Tongue dancing around my mouth as powerful words try to ease between my teeth
But all that comes out is "Blah" as my mind dances in the middle of the street like the people high off life
Oh, how I loved the sweet taste of Manhattan

Rent so high that Manhattan made me homeless
Drowning in Manhattan as people walk by smelling like orange peels
I rise off the speckled concrete as perfume sprays of euphoria dances across my face
I faint as I see my favorite celebrity walk past
You may have ruined my life
But I love you,
Manhattan.

Ch 3: Woke

How is God always as near as a whisper but no one has ever seen him in person. I used to be someone who believed in the tooth fairy, Santa Claus, Peter Pan, and much more. But when I found out they didn't exist (aka when I was told they didn't exist), I was left with one more of these mystical creatures, Jesus. What about him? I was never told that he didn't exist and so many people believed that this was a higher power who held all the ability to guide and help you live in purpose. He was one of those mystical creatures I held on to. However, that was just until I found my life crumbling underneath a higher power, who, I thought, was supposed to protect me. Therefore, I questioned who he is, and where he is.

Only when life went crumbling is when I found myself walking in my truth. I found myself falling victim to a time when eating, sleeping, or any other daily functions was a challenge to me. There was one incident that drove my questioning of this higher power. When I thought Jesus would protect me from all evil and harm that tried to get a hold of my life, he didn't. The same humanity that people say he created is the same humanity that was breaking me. Moreover, I still tried to hold on to my faith by telling myself that the beauty of it all comes at a cost.

If God was always as near as a whisper, then he was there when I popped 19 pills all at once trying to end my life. If God was always as near as a whisper, then he was there when I had fallen so hard that my concussion caused me to temporarily lose my vision. Maybe that's the problem, he is always as near as a whisper, but does nothing to protect. They say, "He's trying to give you a lesson so that you can learn something." But to me, it was like he was giving me a bunch of lessons, but didn't know how to teach.

God supposedly saves people and protects them, and he was supposed to save me too. But, he left me for dead and that was the day I began to stop believing. Then someone told me "well, maybe you weren't supposed to be saved." But I thought that if I wasn't supposed to be saved, then why was I created in the first place? That was a question that I believed that no one can answer except with assumptions or opinions. However, there is a saying that when people assume things, they make an ass out of you and me. My purpose had begun to die.

As I continued to question the existence of this higher power, I began to question what was the difference between me and this mystical creature that everyone praised so highly. Why was he put on a pedestal? If anything, I thought that I was a God to myself because through all my hardships and obstacles when this Jesus turned his back, it was me who got myself through it. It was during a crisis in my life when I questioned the existence of a higher power, and I had written the poem titled "Woke."

Woke

Welcome to my life
I'll expose myself
I can't sleep
I can't eat
I keep tripping over my feet
Because the shoes that I wear
Are filled with hurt and grief
And when I fall, I die inside
My life is like a leaf
Where I get eaten, cut and crumbled
With my pieces stuck in their teeth
This is defeat
I'm incomplete
Because the God that gave me life
Just watches as I deplete

I feel Cheated
Scammed
Heated
Damned
Cuz I'll be damned if praise a god
That will watch as I get rammed
This is my world
Welcome to it
I'll guide you through it
But careful not to fall cuz getting up,
I don't know how to do it
Woke

Somethings been festering deep down in my soul
Who is this Jesus

This god
This hope
This faith
This fear
This book
This joke

But you keep reading
About a man who was broke
A story that was a joke
A promise that was a hoax
My life is a joke
And I wrote a book about it too
Where I live as king
Do I get praise too?
I broke many times
And I rose like him
I've healed a lot of people
And took steps to every hymn

Higher power?
But a human wrote the book
And if I were to write my own
Then they'd give me a certain look
How dare they stare and give me questionnaires
Like I can't compare to the man that's upstairs
That they created but I'm hated
But somehow he's liberated
If you ask me he's outdated.
Cuz I'm here now
And I feel underrated

I'm consciously killing myself

Scratch that
My conscious is killing myself
So forgive me if I fanaticize about being gone today
Because my tomorrow just promised I won't live another day
And as I walk to my tomorrow
My back has a lot of weight
Having anxiety attacks
Because I get yet another day

I'm the type of player you press eject on
I'm the type of man you believers reflect on
Cuz I press on, like press-ons
That fall off, but press on

Persist?
Have you ever seen Jesus? No
But you believe he still exists?
But somehow I'm blind
Because I can't see Jesus
But you can't either
But somehow I'm a heathen

If I'm honest with them, they won't think highly of me
Everything they want me to be is what I'm dying to be
Everything I'm not trying to be
Every time I pop a pill I feel suicide dancing down my throat
Deep into my stomach to poison my gut feeling
High as a kite
As my outer shell starts peeling

Opening up like this is a moment far from my proudest
Voice playing on repeat in my head but it's far from its loudest

Demons keep pressing me but I've become comfortable with their presence
How do I teach in this life with a world full of lessons?

I was a wrong turned right
The last man standing
Who rose with shackles and weights
With wake's on wake's
And seeing death on skates

This life is dead
Cuz this god aint save you
I just woke from my nap
And I'm ready for take 2
Woke

CH 4: Peace Be Still

Peace does not exist outside of your inner being. People have spent decades and centuries trying to achieve world peace, but no such thing exists. Peace can only be achieved within your own self. However, it becomes a dangerous life when peace within yourself cannot be reached. When this happens, people often convey the problem as life instead of themselves, even though life has and will always be chaotic.

There was a time in my life when I could not achieve inner peace, and I was living in chaos trying to find purpose. Then, there was a day where I observed that chaos was not only riveting throughout my life, but numerous people around me. These were people who I was able to understand their current position but could not help them because the broken advising the breaking will only result in brokenness.

Over time it would appear as if time has not changed. This is because the aspect of achieving peace outside of ourselves has not changed. In the process, people have become helpless, hopeless, and unidentifiable. Thousands have given up, and their dying wishes are their desires to fade away with time.

During the time when my life seemed to have gone crumbling and chaos was dancing throughout every day of my life, a friend of mine had just begun struggling with the early stages of depression. His external circumstances had begun poisoning his inner self. Unknowledgeable about how to control his mental state, the essence of his ill mind was controlling the way his thoughts perceived certain interactions and circumstances. He became convinced that happiness was a thing of the past, but there was still hope for peace. However, that was just until he realized that peace did not plan on returning from vacation anytime soon during this critical period of his life.

Then, one night I had been working on an essay and preparing for a final that was to occur the very next day. He had walked into the room and I had observed a drastic shift in his mood. He had seemed more down and mentally checked-out than he had ever been before. I had immediately recognized this familiar feeling and asked him if he was ok. At first, he did not respond. Then, I asked what was going on and if he wanted to talk about it. He said that everything was fine, and he wanted to be left alone. I had told him that whenever he was ready to talk, I was available because I had planned on staying up all night to finish my work that was due the next day. Hours had passed, and it was exactly 3 am. He had not slept and had been laying there on his phone not speaking since our last conversation. At 3 a.m., he said "I'm depressed."

I responded, "I know. It was written all over your face. I was waiting for you to say something. I knew it would come out eventually."

He took the opportunity to vent and get everything off his chest at 3 in the morning. He was teary-eyed and had begun talking about how he is depressed and other outside circumstances that were fuelling the fall of his mental health. His language made me believe that he was falling into the realm of suicidal ideations. Our conversation continued until 6:30 the next morning. I stayed in the room the entire day because I was fearful of leaving him alone. However, I had to leave for about an hour for a presentation I had the next day. After the presentation, I returned to the room and upon trying to open the door, I noticed that it was locked. This was unordinary because the door was never locked because neither one of us had a key to access it, therefore we had the locking mechanism taped so we would not get locked out. As a result, I double-knocked on the door to see if my roommate was in the room; I got no response. I double-knocked again and still received no response. Then for a final time, I knocked again just to make sure, but I got no response. It was at this moment I began to panic because I sensed that something was wrong.

I called my roommate to see if he would answer the phone but there was no answer. I called him once more after that but he still did not pick up. Our room was on the second floor which means that I could crawl out the window onto the roof top to go over to my room window. I considered doing that until I realized that I wasn't that tactical. After this realization, I decided to call one last time before I had to go to get a master key to unlock the door. He answered. He said, "What Gibbs?"

I responded, "Can you let me in the room?"

He said, "What do you want? Did you think I was going to kill myself?"

I responded, "What. Not at all. I just want to get into the room." Even though that was exactly what crossed my mind at the time.

He opened the door and when I walked in I saw a giant spool of 550 cord unravelled all over the floor. I looked at my roommate and asked if he was ok. Irritably, he responded, "I'm fine Gibbs!"

I told him, "Well, I'll be here when you are ready to talk."

After that moment, I never left the room and was very cautious about leaving him alone even when I went to the bathroom. Hours pass by and he finally tells me what had happened. All I could think was thank God I was there at the right moment because who knows what could have happened if I had arrived a little later.

This incident made me realize the extremes we will go to achieve peace. So much chaos was going on throughout my roommate's life and mine, and it made me wonder what would it be like if peace was achievable or if peace was still for at least a moment in time. If we could yell "Peace be still!" and every single time all chaos that was riveting throughout our lives would halt, then could this life that we fight so hard to live end in purpose? We were at a point where the want for peace was great but the gap to achieve it was even greater.

Through this lifelong search for peace, we often think of what we can do to change ourselves. However, most of the time these are just thoughts that are not acted upon. Then, we develop this delusion that we are making progress because we are thinking about changing, but in reality we have not progressed.

We often ask who we identify with or identify as but seldom do we respond with our own name. When we name other people who we aspire to be, we often disregard ourselves which implies that we are not good enough. Life is a constant journey to find ourselves, peace, and comfort in life. When someone else's pain makes us feel uncomfortable, we often reach out to them. One of the reasons we do this is because his or her pain is causing a disruption of our own inner peace.

All in all, this poetic incident and interpretation of peace, caused me to write "Peace, Be still."

Peace, Be Still

Through decades of time, and I still see no changes
Making helpless minds who wish they were nameless
If you want to be great, then you've got to be shameless
Cuz life is live for even those who aren't famous

Hundreds of people dying with tattoos of suicide
But no focus on the issue of finding who's inside
Of them wanting passionate pain to pleasure their lies
Confused by the blues so their making a noose tie

And I can still see the passionate pain in someone's eyes
Wishing for much better days and bluer skies
And sometimes skies are black and clouds cry
But when it's raining tears, a flower feels good inside

Peace would run so fast that the mind would penalize
And I used to run track, so yea I can sympathize
Yelling PEACE BE STILL!! So your mind won't criminalize
Your thoughts barred from the great escape to realize

Peace be still
Peace be still
Everybody stand together and yell "Peace be still!!"
Cuz when the tough is not going and going isn't tough
Saying "Please be still" may not be enough

Peace be still frozen in time
I thought about a change but my change didn't mind
Still pressing my buttons and stuck in rewind
So I still thought progress and the allusion of refined

Cuz I'm frozen in time and peace is still running
And thought if peace was still then that would be stunning
But the thought was a thought and my clout would fade away
So I'm praying to believe that peace would save me from this day

Yelling PEACE BE STILL!! So the frozen would sun
And the sun would thaw and the time would run
And that peace would stop, and the time would come
That I hum with the hymns of holiness

Peace be still like the hair of a Who
So when I cut my thoughts, they wouldn't bleed blue
So I can be the chosen one plus one like two
Cents that no one wants cuz my mind isn't you

I'll levitate to meditate so that peace be still
I'll space out and gravitate so that peace be still
I'll step up to escalate so that peace be still
I'll press on to elevate so that peace be still
Because when the tough is not going
And going isn't tough
Saying "Please be still" may not be enough

CH. 5: Running

I always get to where I'm going by walking away from where I've been. You can't move into the future while being stuck in the past. Problems are subjective to your thinking. I found myself running away from the past and general things I've identified as a problem. So, instead of dealing with these issues, I would run away from them and hope that they would eventually fade away or disappear. I've ran away from home and never looked back. I've run from the past that contained all my problems hoping to get far away from them. I've ran from reality because to face it would only bring the pain I've been trying to get away from. The problem with this is that, occasionally, the past will come back to haunt. We will eventually face things that are similar to the things we tried to run from, and we don't know how to deal with it or move forward because we never took the time to deal with it before. Therefore, along the way when we are trying to get to where we are going, we trip, stumble, and fall along the way.

There was a time where I ran so far away from home that I didn't know what home was. By home, I'm referencing a mindset, not necessarily a physical place. My conscience was lost, and my ability to be comfortable within my own self was jeopardized. A long journey was ahead in finding where my home was. My journey then became a search for this place that I had desired so much. If home is where the heart was, then my heart would have been lost. What do we say to the person who's pain in life stems from the one place he or she spent much of his or her life living? Shall we say welcome home? Welcome home to where your burdens lie and push you out into this life where you are lost and losing. Welcome home to where the first break in your life fueled so many other ones. Welcome home to where the most pleasant and the most hurtful moments can gain life again. Welcome home.

What do we say to the people where a broken home is the only home that they know of? Numerous lives are spent running from this place to find another one. But, the problem with this is that we never look to handle or heal the brokenness, and instead we leave it behind in hopes to find a new home with less brokenness. However, wherever we go, we are subconsciously carrying all the things that caused us to be broken with us to our new home. We end up handling obstacles in the same way that further long our hurting. It comes a point in time when we must stop running and finally face what we all have been running from.

There was a time in my life that I spent running from all the things that hurt me or caused me to have a significant life impact. I ran in hopes to not let it return into my future. I figured if I ran long and far enough, I would never have to worry about it again. Particularly, there was a time in my life where I had lost a close friend. I did not know how to cope with this, and then it had occurred again. It was in this moment when I had become distancing myself from all friendships and relationships. I had convinced myself that if I had not been close to these people in the first place I could have avoided being heart-broken. As a result, I had run from all relationships that could make me vulnerable to being hurt again. I never reached out to anyone in times of hurt, I stopped valuing friendships, and I ran so far from these relationships that I lost myself.

Because of this type of thinking, I became lonely, depressed, and had no one to talk to in my extreme times of need. In the end, it ended up hurting me more than it helped. I had to progressively stop running from the problems that I avoided facing. In the times I ran from my problems, I always found myself constantly tripping and stumbling along the way while trying to find a new home to forget the past. But soon enough the past would come back to haunt, and when it did, I left myself with two choices. Either I die this way, or I face it. I made the conscious decision to face it and stop running. And it was only when I had stopped running and faced my past burdens, is when I was finally able to find a place I can call home and progress in life. It's hard to heal in your future without healing from your past.

Running

If there was a place I could relax
That I could call home
I wouldn't run from the past
Or trip over stones
Wouldn't jog from reality
Or feel quite alone
Wouldn't walk from problems
If there was a place called home

I've ran so far that there is no time to look back
I've tripped, stumbled, and fell along the way
I've been physically and mentally, abused and attacked
I'm running, I'm running, I'm running away
From reality I'm running in order to cope
From past to future to problems and hope
I'm running, I'm running in order to cope
I'm running, I'm running, I'm running from hope

Standing on mountains looking into the distance
Drying my eyes and lifting my head
For those see me, I wish them good riddance
I'm physically smiling and emotionally dead

I cut down trees that block my light
I look behind me and see the sun coming my way
I bless the stars that twinkle in darkness
But still jogging and jogging, I'm jogging away?
From reality I'm jogging in order to cope
From past to future to problems and hope
I'm jogging, I'm jogging in order to cope
I'm jogging, I'm jogging, I'm jogging from hope

Moving forward at all times
Erasing my path along the way
Catching up, the sun is above me
A beaming light coming my way
From reality I'm walking in order to cope
From past to future to problems and hope
I'm walking, I'm walking in order to cope
I'm walking, I'm walking, I'm walking from hope

I look ahead and see darkness
I peek behind and see light
I start to slow for hope
I begin to halt to fight
For reality I'm stopping in order to hope
From past to future to problems and hope
I'm stopping, I'm stopping in order to hope
I'm stopping, I'm stopping, I'm stopping for hope

I've ran, I've coped, I've stopped, I've hoped
I've tripped, I've fell, I've fought, I've yelled
I'm here with tears with scars and years
I'm back, in pain, I'm home, I came

There is a place I can relax
That I can call home
I don't run from the past
Or trip over stones
Don't jog from reality
Or feel quite alone
Don't walk from problems
Cuz there is a place called home

CH. 6: Praying

When there is nothing left, all you can do is pray. When I had lost all resources including faith, I prayed for hope. Hope had been lost when I hit rock bottom for the first time. But what we don't realize is that when we hit rock bottom the only way to go is up. Given up and weak, I had become a broken man. The one thing I prayed for was hope. When a broken man says healing happens, there is much power in his voice. Hope has the ability to take us a long way; we have to make sure it's the right way.

Prayer is the key that unlocks the gates of hope and closes the gates of despair. A prayer is a request; a request for a type of healing that only a higher power can provide. However, for me, praying served as a coping strategy to deal with my emptiness. I also viewed praying as something I did when I did not believe in myself enough to make it through certain circumstances. Ultimately, it was a request for a need I could not fulfil.

Oftentimes, people say think outside the box, or that people get to where they are going by thinking outside the box. My question is who the person is who created this box. I believe society created this box to limit people's thinking in order to make sure that "we all don't make it" because if we all make it, none of us do. The box was created to keep the people who they know will fall victim to this box inside. So, my response is that I no longer live or think in a world where boxes exist. There is no box for me to think inside of.

There had come a time in my life when I experienced multiple losses of close ones within one-month, precancerous lesions in my abdomen, and financial instability all at the same time. It was during this moment where I had begun thinking there is no way out of here. I thought that if this is my life, then I did not want it. So as one of my last resorts, I had begun praying in hopes that someone will answer my prayer or at least provide me with a direction because, quite frankly, I was lost. However, during this time, I had lost faith in life and in myself, so as a result, my praying turned into a coping strategy rather than a healing.

During this critical time, there were people in my life that I had to distance myself from due to toxicity. These were people who made attempts to put me down in my low moments instead of uplifting me. These were what I would call dream killers because they work hard to set you back on your movement forward. These are people that you avoid telling good news too because they will try to do or say things to bring discredit to the one thing that is bringing you joy in your life. However, I soon realized that what other people say about you or even do, is none of your business. This is because when you walk your path fearless with God's grace, there is nothing that no other human being on earth can do to stop you because it is your destiny. I learned to rise to the occasion almost every time; however, sometimes I fell, but I fell forward. And overtime, I had become more and more willing to fall in order to be mentally prepared to receive my blessing when it comes.

Even though I had begun questioning life so much during this time, I still believed that life was nothing but another form of cryptocurrency; anyone can create it, and you define its value. No matter how much I am beaten down, no matter how much I break, I will still have value. That is something that no one can take from you except yourself. However, when you feel like you have no value is when we tend to fall victim to poor mental health and develop an inability to rise through adversity. I was willing to die of the complete form I was in, in order to birth the man I was becoming. I subconsciously knew that there was something in store for me, I just had trouble realizing what it was and how to find it. As a result, I prayed more often and wrote the poem "Praying" to passionately help me realize my worth and that because I am able to survive my circumstances, I will be able to increase in value over time.

Praying

I've been longing for hope
I've been beat, bamboozled, and broke
I've given up
On my knees, head shaking
Tears flowing
Heart Showing
Praying...
for a sprinkle of hope

So I cope
And I cope
And I cope
And I cope
Because I'm broke
With a heart of gold
Praying and longing for hope

To hear a broken man say healing happens
A man who breaks, but breaks by snapping
A man who hides, but hides by laughing
A man who breathes in the breeze that's trapping
Thoughts
Praying...
for a sprinkle of hope

I can see that I am treasure
Because I am blessed beyond measure
Pushing still
Standing still
Prospering still
Because my cracks has been filled with gold

And my tears are written in bold
I'm alone and afraid
So, all I can do is pray
for a sprinkle of hope

And so I cope
And I cope
And I cope
And I cope
Because I'm broke
With a heart of gold
Praying and longing for hope

Enemy aiming at my head
To put me to rest with no bed
Wanting the blood that I don't shed
Feeling blue but I'm red
With white flags
Praying
for a sprinkle of hope

Ready to shoot me into a coffin
But when aimed, they started coughing
Cuz no weapon formed against me shall prosper
No weapon formed against me shall prosper
That's why I'm still standing
Undefeated and succeeded
No holes and completed
But feeling as if I lost
Praying
for a sprinkle of hope

And so I cope

And I cope
And I cope
Because I'm broke
With a heart of gold
Praying and longing for hope

Keep praying on my downfall
And yelling "get down!!" "Fall!!"
So I rise to the occasion
So I can rise through the occasion
But my conscience says I should not have risen to that at all
And so I pray
for a sprinkle of hope

And so I cope
And I cope
And I cope
And I cope
And I cope
And I cope
And I cope
And I cope
Because I'm broke
With a heart of gold
Praying and longing for hope

I tried to tell them but they run away
That why I'm still standing here today
Because what God bless no man can curse
That why I'm doing better, and they're doing worst
Breaking down in numerous attempts
Trying so shrink me to that of a shrimp
But I pray

for a sprinkle of hope

I am a saint and a sinner
I'm a loser and a winner
I'm a snack and a dinner
My light shines and it glimmers
I'm a mess
Praying
For a sprinkle of hope

And so I cope
And I cope
And I cope
Because I'm broke
With a heart of gold
Praying and longing for hope

I've made it this far on my own
Once young and now grown
Once burrowed and now loans
Once fleshed and now bones
Trying to muscle through
Praying
for a sprinkle of hope

I've mad terrible decisions
The devil had me in cuffs
Life ready to be given
But I'm a diamond in the rough
With the keys to be released
But I fear floors that are greased
And so I pray
for a sprinkle of hope

And so I cope
And I cope
And I cope
And I cope
And I cope
Because I'm broke
With a heart of gold
Praying and longing for hope

I went to sleep when the world was cold
So frozen that I began to mold
And I woke when it was on fire
I was thawing but I was tired
Of life
Dying but not dead yet
Alive but not live yet
Praying...
People dying at the hands of the enemy
So in their hands, they rest in chaos
But living in the hands of the lord
So in his hands they rest in peace
Feeling designer wounds in LV
Feeling damaged hearts in VA
Feeling blood in my oranges
Praying
for peace, prosperity, and hope

And so I cope
And I cope
And I Cope
And I COpe
And I COPe

And I COPE
AND I COPE
AND I COPE
AND I COPE
AND I COPED!!
So I broke
With a heart of gold
Praying.

CH. 7: I'm Sorry

I had to become willing to be my own rescue at the risk of other people's approval. There was someone that I had known in my life whose own life was lived through other people's approval. Everything that was done was done always for other people, and never his own self. If there is anyone who is like this, there will soon come a time where you will have to be your own approval. No matter what walk of life you are from, there will always be someone somewhere who will have an opinion about who you are, or what you do. However, we must realize that these opinions are just the thoughts of human beings and nothing more. We all have our own thoughts, but when we change ourselves to conform to the mindsets of others, we subconsciously devalue our own thoughts and ourselves. We are saying to ourselves that we are not good enough to accept the way we are created. No single person's thought is better than the next. We all think in different ways, but when we compare ourselves to the majority or to what is accepted, we dilute our own thoughts that make us unique. I am not here on earth to seek acceptance, I am here to show what I have to offer. And if I so happen to make an impact or positive change in the process, then kudos to me.

Early December, that someone that I had known ended up taking his life. I had not known what was going on or why he did this. But I can assume that his thoughts had become too much for him to handle. I assume that he thought his circumstances were too great to overcome. I assume his current position in life was not favorable in his mind. And I can assume that these were the thoughts that took his own life. He fell into the dark hole in his mind that thought frequently he was not good enough. It was heart-breaking because everyone thought he would go far, but no one thought he would go this far. This ended up being a life that could have been saved. This was a life that could have been changed. This was a life that could have seen the little sparkles in a dark world. But what I am about to say may differ from most people's opinions, but it needs to be said. If he could hear me, I would tell him that what he did was not selfish. The people who say suicide is a selfish act most of the time had never known what it would be like to attempt to take their own life. However, as hard as it is to accept, he did fight hard to overcome. I'm sure there was hesitation because there was a battle in his mind occurring between conflicting thoughts. But, the thoughts that you give power to win in the end.

My message to those who have or are experiencing something like this, is I'm sorry. I'm sorry that you feel alone, and that what you are experiencing seems too great to overcome. I'm sorry that you may have a life full of regrets. I'm sorry that the person you may have asked for help wasn't able too. I'm sorry that someone may have took time out of his or her life to try to ruin yours; but they lost time while you gained yet another opportunity to grow stronger. I'm sorry that you feel like your success, goals, or aspirations in life cost too much. I'm sorry you feel like God had turned his back on you, and that you feel taking your life is the only option you have left. On behalf of myself and all the other people who would like to unify to bring awareness to mental health, I am sorry. Life is like a marathon, you run too fast, you'll eventually burn out, and if you run too slow, you just might lose the race. But fast or slow, win or lose, to finish is to make it through all obstacles regardless of its severity; run at your own pace. Your loss affects me only if I let it. To know that I have once felt what it feels like to give up, quit, or stop this ongoing race, and to know that I have survived, and someone else did not, it makes me wonder if I could have saved someone's life. What I realized is that I felt comfortable being at the bottom because my growth is inevitable. I also realized that maybe I just have never failed, I just found thousands of ways that won't work, and life is just a marathon looking for the one way that will. I, too, was a victim of unfortunate circumstances and suicidal thoughts. I, too, have been through hell and back took a detour through heaven only to end up back in hell once more. However, despite the odds, I used my drive to get even, I used my drive to find balance, and I used every unwanted circumstance as reason to keep it pushing because it's someone out there that couldn't. I want to prove to the world that there is a way even in the roughest parts of life.

We can all make it if we want to, but that's only if the subconscious want not to isn't greater. I am here to inform you that the "not good enough" mindset must go. Every time someone takes their life, there is something in their head that implies that he or she was not good enough. Not being good enough stems from a comparison to other ideas or human beings that bleed the same way we all do. When your success isn't defined by a comparison to other people, nothing can stop you. I may have been at rock bottom, almost didn't make it, but I turned my pain into pleasure and developed the craving to rise despite the odds pinned against me. I took every stone that was thrown my way and decided to build an empire. I learned to conquer this place in my head even when it felt like all I had was myself. I am also here to inform you that you can always use an ill mind to your advantage. And when there are people who try to block you from continuing your journey, when there are people who laugh at your struggle, when there are people who watch you from a distance afraid to get near you, only you will determine who will get the last laugh. And I want that laugh and burst of happiness with a few giggles to spare. Wise isn't always the one who makes it to the end, it can be the one who uses their circumstances to create a new beginning.

I'm Sorry

I'm lost
Now that I've lost you
I'm lost
Because the cost was you
I'm lost
Now that you're through
I'm lost
Because I lost you
I'm sorry

After preaching so much on how to survive the storm
My life is full of regrets because I didn't get to you in time
When you screamed for me to help you from drowning
I didn't hear you in time
And now it's pulling me under
I'm sorry.

It's not many who can break me
But you broke my heart
Because you were there from the start
And even though I feel like we fell apart
You're a part of this journey I'm about to embark
I'm sorry

Now that I have lost you
It is affecting my health
Now that I have lost you
I've lost my wealth
Now that I have lost you
I've lost myself

I'm lost
In a world where the masses preach success is going to cost you
It comes with a price that is bigger than most are willing to pay
BUT IF I HAD KNOWN THE COST WAS GOING TO BE YOU
I would have never gave anything away
I'm sorry

You're on my mind
You're on my mind
Make it stop God
But if you were in my position
Would you stop God?
All this poison in my head
Make it stop God
Why you always seem to take?
Why mine God?
Please don't take anyone else
Take me god
Because I can't take the pain
But I tried hard

It's like you looked up at me for some help
But I was too busy trying to heal myself
And now you're too far to reach and I'm in hell
I feel like you're in jail with no bail in a cell
I'm sorry

Now you are another name added to the list
I knew if I'd told Sean he would be pissed
But he's there too and now you're both missed
I hear your mind screaming and it sounds like this

I'm overdosing and over coasting on these pills
Put it in drive
Speed up
This is a drill
I feel like I'm about to take what's mine
Because my sun don't shine
And miss the light with the lime
Is it time?
Is it time?!
to aim and kill
For a breath of fresh air
And put the deed on my bill
To feel the blood in my hair
This isn't fair
Cuz the air that I breathe isn't clear
And the thoughts that say no isn't here
I'm sorry

You know I can hear the words now
And it's haunting my mind
Because when you thought that you were running late
It wasn't your time
God Damn!!
I wish that I was there to take the gun away
Because my heart is about to fail because your gone away
And now that I'm the last one standing I don't want to stay
And if I had gone back in time I would just fade away

I'm lost in this world looking for the reason I breathe
But all these losses in this world is going to be the reason I leave
And I hope that your way won't be the way that I grieve

Because my fate in this world is going to be the fate that I dream
I'm sorry

This life is full of pain and hurt
Where we all struggle trying to figure out what pain is worth
And if you feel you're worth less than your pain is burnt
Because the match can't light after the pain's been burnt

Why did you take your life?
Did it seem right?
You lost the fight
So you ran
Right into my life

And now I'm about to crash
I hear my thoughts ringing
But your thoughts already here
Cuz I can hear them singing
My heart pounding out my chest
Because you keep drilling
Now it's too hard to heal
Because my blood is spilling

I can hear them now whispering inside my head
Give up, go sleep, you can use my bed
Put the knife to your wrist
Hold the pills in your fist
Add your name to this list
And you'll soon be the mist
I'm sorry

Would you be satisfied if I put a bullet in my eyes?

To take the pain away or find joy in my demise
Or are these lies?
Because I feel there's pieces missing to my pie
What's the use of hi if we never say goodbye
I'm sorry

See you can't light a match if it's burnt
So you aint on fire
You aint lit,
And you aint turnt
And if it's not today
When will you people start to learn?
That it is never over when the meeting's just adjourned

And if you feel you can't do it
Just ask somebody else
And if you don't care about nothing
At least care about yourself
I'm sorry

Phase 2:

Depression

CH. 8: Every Night

I had found myself lying in bed full of depression because I had lost control of my feelings and my life. It had become routine for me to have random breakdowns, but most of them occurred when I took the time to lay in bed and think about my circumstances. I had gotten used to staying up for most of the night because my mind could never relax enough for me to sleep. And oftentimes, the only time I would finally fall asleep is if I cried my eyes out for a long period of time until my eyes got eventually too heavy to keep them open. I spent days trying to regain control and figure out why I'm feeling the way I did. I had felt weak, helpless, and worthless. But the truth is that I was fearful of my circumstances that would determine my future. Nights had become so restless that I would have to take a lot of melatonin in order to go to sleep. Furthermore, sometimes when I did finally fall asleep, I would oftentimes have night terrors of past experiences and potential future experiences. It was after these moments that I had begun to enter through the gates of depression.

I had numbed my feelings so much that I had become heartless. I had stopped caring for my inner being and started to keep things bottled up. I would pretend that none of the hardships I was going through affected me emotionally. I had no longer become scared of death, in fact, I became ok if I were to never wake up again. I was broken. But the problem wasn't in that I was broken; the problem was that my brokenness kept breaking. I saw no sign of healing coming my way. However, in this constant search for peace and healing, I realized that the search itself was a sign that even though I am depressed, I am still actively looking for ways to heal the pain that resides deep within me. In this sense, I realized that I was fighting despite the negative emotions that I would take to bed with me every night.

Every night I went to bed feeling the heat of my past experiences. I constantly thought "what if?" What if this is my last time falling asleep? What if none of this is actually happening and it is all a dream? What if I wake up and a miracle happens and all my problems are fixed? But it was these very questions that were leading to my demise. Take notice that none of them implied that I actually face my issues. When I actually did sleep I would have nightmares and night terrors about the past damaging my future. I would have nightmares of people doing everything in their power to ensure my demise; moreover, this was happening in real life. I had a nightmare that I was in a position that a lie would hold more weight than the truth; I was in that position in real life. However, no matter how much weight a lie has, it will always be defenseless against the truth. Harmful things from other people shall not have power over me. I had a hard time realizing this. All I saw was my nightmares coming to real life, and because of this, I no longer wanted this real life experience.

Because of this nightly experience, I had begun losing a sense of my worth. I believed that I was not valuable. I was too broken to be worth anything. The mental pain I had been experiencing came to a point where it couldn't hurt anymore because I had become numb. It seemed to me that the pain I had experienced was on a mission in which I had no idea what the outcome was going to be. I just believed it wasn't going to work in my favor. However, soon enough I would realize that this pain I was experiencing every night I went to bed was supposed to teach me a life lesson. It was a blessing in disguise because it gave me an experience that I could pass to other people, which made my story much more powerful.

Every night it felt like I was on a stage and when I approached the edge, my brain would always tell me to step back. I think this happened because before I fall, I either have done it before or saw someone else do it. My mind is signalling to me that I will get hurt; however, if I never take the risk, I will never know what it's like to experience life beyond the edges.

Oftentimes, I asked myself what kept me going or what kept me alive? And then I realized that when I get old in a rocking chair, I am going to tell the story of my life; but when I am young, I am making sure that story is going to be good to tell. And this was why I chose to keep going.

Every Night

Every night I cry to sleep
Because honestly
I can't figure out why I'm weak
And then I weep
Throughout the week
Until I pill myself to sleep

I can't feel with all this heat
What's a heart without its beat
And if death is only sleep
Can I sleep?
To get through the week

Self-love is pain
Self-love is weak
And if my self is broken
Then my love is beat
My self is broke and beat
Like broken beats
In broken hearts
That breaks and weeps
I'm beat with a beat heart that's weak

Should I ask the body of death to give me life again
To Kill my soul so I can restart this life of sin
Because it's been tough in hell
fighting a battle I can't win

I understand the thoughts of suicide
That do reside
That do imply

that I will feel the heat of all my past

I don't know my worth no more
It can't get worse no more
Because I've hurt so much
That it can't hurt no more

This pain is sufficient
This pain is on a mission
This pain is winning
This pain is living

Listen
I hate to see my own reflection
Praying for an intervention
This natural selection
Or survival of the fittest

I can feel it in my chest
I can feel it in flesh
The only way it will leave
Is if I choose death

So God if you can hear me
Please set me free
And if not lord
Can you just let me leave?

Because every night
I dream this dream
And every night
I cry to sleep
Weak

CH. 9: Fade Away

If I had the power to go back in time and change anything, I would've said take it all away. I noticed that I had not truly lived life unless a life of pain was the type of life I lived. A life of pain is one that I did not want. I felt dead and lifeless, so I thought to myself what was the point of still suffering every day. This feeling of pain was one that took a severe toll on my brain. As a result, my mind went through many roller coasters and emotions. There was nothing more that I wanted at this point in time but to take it all away. Take this life away where I go to sleep with the regret of waking up. The want to give up on life lurks deep inside my soul and creates mental storms that leaves me with devastating effects. Life has become lifeless, and I watch a piece of my soul fade away with every breath I take. It feels as though my mind has run its course, and is in a casket ready to be buried forever. But, as I carry the casket to my final resting place, each step becomes heavier and my arms begin to tremble. This is when I realize that the smallest caskets are the hardest to carry. I longed for a break, but life doesn't offer those. Something was stopping me and slowing me down, but soon enough I realized that I am carrying this casket alone. I was alone at my own funeral that I created in an attempt to bury myself. My thoughts constantly reminded me that I am not living; this is not the life you were created to live. So in these moments, I tried to end it rather than becoming willing to make a change. I knew I had to become willing, but that willingness fell victim to the wrong thought.

Depressingly, I had become more willing for suicide rather than a significant life change. I had ups where I thought it would get better, and I had downs where my circumstances chose me to be a victim. Soon enough, I noticed that even though I thought I was lifeless, it was quite the opposite. I realized that I felt every single feeling that was imparted upon my mind, body, and soul, however, this made me feel "too alive". I did not understand that the beauty of life, if you shall call it that, comes with both feelings of happiness and deep despair. I had trouble accepting that.

If love knows no boundaries, then what should I say to myself? For a period of time, it seemed as if the boundary that was not supposed to exist was me. I have loved many others, so much so, that I would do anything for them not to feel my pain or go through what I have went through. I was willing to die to ensure this. I could not understand why, but I quickly realized that I hated myself so much that I would die a thousand times over so that no one would end up like me. One problem that quickly surfaced with this mindset was that I expected others to do the same for me. After numerous let-downs, I realize that we are not our expectations. But, that did not change the love that I had for all of these people who seemingly failed me in the same way that I had failed myself.

Although we have moments where we crumble, fall-apart, and everything in between, we must not forget to treat ourselves like someone we love. We have to remember that we must reciprocate the amount of love we give to others, especially in times where the want to fade away bombards our minds. Even though life may be painful at times, that pain strengthens us for a change that is long overdue.

Fade Away

If I had gone back in time
I'd say take it all away
If murder asked if he could kill me
I don't know what I'd say
Life is dead, I aint living
My thoughts said every day
If this is what's called pain
I wish I could fade away

I went from thinking it would get better
To thoughts of suicide
From rising through the weather
To feeling blue inside
From writing hope inside some letters
To feeling too alive
My "too alive" thought suicide from feeling blue inside

I would die a thousand deaths so that no one feels my pain
If I had made a great escape then they'd think I was insane
If my life was like art and my brushes were meant to paint
Then I'd just be a canvas with my art stuck in the rain

If I had gone back in time
I'd say take it all away
If murder asked if he could kill me
I don't know what I'd say
Life is dead, I aint living
My thoughts said every day
If this is what's called pain
I wish I could fade away

If the heart is a Muscle
My muscles would be weak
So weak, that it leaks
And you could see it in my cheeks
It aches from the pain cuz everyday it has to beat
But if my muscle were to give, I won't be in pain another week

Not red, but black
So I could feel less
My heart less
I'm heartless
So I hurt less and love less

Cuz life gets dark and from the pain I feel sore
If my heart stops, let me rest, so that it don't hurt no more
So sore, SO sore, I can feel it in my core
Cuz my muscle is damaged, from my heart that you just tore

If I had gone back in time
I'd say take it all away
If murder asked if he could kill me
I don't know what I'd say
Life is dead, I aint living
My thoughts said every day
If this is what's called pain
I wish I could fade away

I confided in a friend
And they confided in themselves
I'd fight for 'em till the end
They threw my effort down a well
Even though it was broken

My heart is what I lent
I had given you my all
And your hurt is what you sent

I'd cry for you
I'd die for you
I'd lie for you
I'd try for you
And if I was on my last breath that you needed, I'd sigh for you

If I had gone back in time
I'd say take it all away
If murder asked if he could kill me
I don't know what I'd say
Life is dead, I aint living
My thoughts said every day
If this is what's called pain
I wish I could fade away

CH. 10: Save Me

You can't break a heart that is already broken. With everything that I had experienced, I truly became numb. There was a point in life when a mind full of pain was the new norm for me. No matter how much damage or how many new wounds I had suffered, it all began to feel no different. Once you've become numb, you forget what it feels like to experience pain. This becomes dangerous because this is when you are most vulnerable, and the silent killer sneaks in for the kill. The silent killer was my conscience. It told me so many tales of what I could and could not survive. It identified everything that was supposed to hurt and how much. It came to a point where my conscience became the catalyst for my downfall. I became worrisome that it would be my conscience that would eventually push me one step too far.

My conscience provided a negative for every positive I encountered. The scary thing about this is that my mind gave so much power to the negative, that the positive was becoming less and less notable. After many battles, I realized that I had to overcome this in one way or another. I was becoming my own worst enemy. I was killing myself from the inside out. I fantasized about everything that I wanted in life that was light years away. Essentially, I had to become willing to battle myself in order to conquer and receive the blessings that existed outside of my inner being.

I noticed that as I began to find and learn myself, I had become closer to God. Once I was able to provide for myself, he began to show me that he was there along the way. I had to learn that God does not show up when you want him too; he only shows when he believes you are ready. God was waiting on me, and I used my lack of understanding to fuel the fire that was throwing my conscience out of orbit. Once I started to work with myself, he removed people that were hindering my growth. He gave both me and my enemy lessons to take away from. I watched my enemies fold before my own eyes for going against me as I was growing. I acknowledged that my enemies tried to bury me not knowing that I was a seed. I am God's child, and he was not going to let anything or anyone bring dishonor upon his work. He made it so that every sour tongue did not stand against my will, not even my own. My faulty conscience was the beginning of the end of a journey that I needed.

Once I had become willing to work on myself, I developed the courage to ask God to save me or protect me from my own shortcomings. Indeed, this was the beginning of a process long overdue. With this new outlook on life, I realize that uneasy lies the head that wears the crown. I had to experience this numbness, pain, and battle within myself in order to become king of this life that I was created to live.

Save me

Stab my heart
Puncture my arteries
I've experienced worse
I am still here
Suffering the wounds
Sprinkled with salt
Bleeding red and white out of my blue veins
Save me from my conscience
Before he kills me

I fought and beat all enemies
He turned a friend against me
I wrote my escape and read between the lines
And he wrote suicide
Someone turned my water into wine
And my wine into liquor
God gave me a medical clearing
And he attacked my heart, blood, and stomach
Save me from my conscience
Before he kills me

I think about something I've never seen before
Heaven and light that does not fade
I have been blessed beyond measure
I thank god for removing all enemies from my life
I watched them stumble and vanish for going against me
He made it so that every sour tongue doesn't stand against my will
I am forever thankful
But now, I ask him to save me from my conscience
Before he kills me

He speaks loudly
He shivers my bones
Kill him before he kills me
Save me

CH. 11: Bottled

The feelings that arise from negative energy and thoughts that are silenced becomes yet another message added to the already full bottle that carries me through life. The problem is that these negative messages are stored for later until it can't be stored anymore. The bottle is heavy, but still I carry that weight with me. The bottle is so full that cracks begin to divide the glass. The dangerous part of this is that once this bottle breaks, all those negative thoughts and energy that I stored for later floods my mind all at once. If I keep holding on to extra weight and baggage, this ideology of a broken bottle will lead to my demise. I quickly needed to realize that if I truly wanted to heal from the things that I perceived to have caused me to become damaged, then I must not hold on to the feelings that resulted from those circumstances. It was in this moment that I acknowledged that I cannot solve a problem with the same mind that created it, and I cannot heal from a negative thought with the same methods that made it grow.

Although Maya Angelou says "We may face many defeats, but we shall not be defeated," I was one who believed I was the one exception. I appreciated defeat for the wrong reasons. I appreciated defeat in a way that brought a sensation that made me admire the "I can't do anything about it" mindset. I used this to fuel the thought that since I couldn't do anything about it, I can finally get a break from the agony that was constantly bombarding my conscience. I guess this is what they mean when it is called the sweet taste of defeat.

Sometimes it takes getting beat down and experiencing the feeling of giving up in order to appreciate the rise. Once I have experienced this, I get inspired by the rise, and it is in these moments where I feel like I am living life and living it up. It gives me an indescribable high that no drug or alcohol can provide because I know that because I've been through this feeling once before, I know I can get through it again. It's the feeling of saying that I survived that makes me continue. Because I had survived so much, it inspired many other people that surround me to keep on. It was this feeling that made me realize that we are not really trusted for the things we claim, rather we are trusted for the things we've survived. It is something about people knowing that I had been through it that makes them trust your own ability to live life to the fullest.

All in all, our bottles may be broken, but we are not broken beyond repair. Everything can be fixed if you have the right mind and process to do so. If we can learn to be inspired by the moment whether good or bad, the stress on our minds shall be relieved because when we rise, we rise not only for ourselves but for others who may be watching. We do not die when we break into pieces because pieces can always be put back together. No matter what we go through, and no matter how we break, we are still ourselves, just in a different form. Our lives are a puzzle that is constantly being pieced together. We are like water; water never dies, it only transforms. It may evaporate, freeze, or boil but at the end of every cycle, it will still be water waiting to rain to water someone else's flowers including our own so that we can rise again unbroken and un-bottled.

Bottled

So here we meet again
Face to face
With an unwanted conversation
Flooding my mind with poison
The poem I could never finish
Where light meets dark in the climax of my story
Where Sue was by my side
And left a deep depression where she was standing
She had filled my glass bottle
Full of poison that I had never drank
And now the bottle is breaking
My bottle
Is breaking

Defeat tastes so sweet
Because I get a break like at a creek
And when I peek at the week
My peak feels weak
Cuz I find what I don't seek
And when I meet the week
It knocks me off my feet
And when I lay like I've been beat
Defeat tastes so sweet

You give up to get up
And you live on to live up
High
Or
You get down to lay down
And smile to not frown

But when the weak shall get restless
Then the week shall get restless
Wanting to stress less
But a want to stress less
Will only stress more
And as I begin to crack
My cracks divides the glass
And my bottle
Is breaking

What is lavish?
Because if it is what I say it is
A blessing in disguise
A triumph over demise
Living in truth over lies
Then lavishness must come at a cost
Because I'm broke
Bottled
Choked
Startled!!
Because my glass that's half full
Is broken
And its emptiness gives me satisfaction
Broke and
Bottled

CH. 12: Dear Depression

Though I suffer from depression amongst many other things, I accept that suicide is not the answer. Suicide is a permanent solution to a temporary problem. Even though problems may have permanent damage, it is what you do with the experience of that problem that is important. We shall not be victims of our circumstances nor shall we be victims of things we cannot control. No one was promised a problem-free life, in fact, everyone will experience a time where they will feel sad or discouraged. The sadness validates the value of what you lost, but it is not always about what you've lost; it's about what you have gained along the way. Depression is a boomerang because it always seems to come back; I had just become better at dealing with it although nothing much about the feeling itself has changed.

There was a point in my life experience where I was not living life for the sake of living life, instead I was living to die. There were moments in which I longed for this life sentence to end. Essentially, I was waiting on a period. During the times when I tried to make it end, there was hesitation with every single moment. The hesitation meant that I had a desire to see where things go. I kept pushing because I maintained this desire. The only issue with this is what happens when I lose this desire.

My relationship with depression was one that I wanted to falter like many others in my life. Essentially, I needed a break-up to happen in order to rid myself of the painful memories that coincided with this union. I sought to forget about this relationship once it was over, but somehow we just ended up back together. Depression was one who held me tight, oftentimes against my will.

Dear Depression

Can you just lie to me?
To ruin our vibe
To ruin these memories
I got to forget
Somehow
And a permanent fix is not the way

I'm begging you to burn our relationship to the ground
I know it's over
So help me get over you
Tell me you like somebody else
Or something
But I don't want to wish poison upon anyone
I need a reason to move on
A reason to hate you
A reason to let it go
Cuz with you I can't live on

You hold me tight and never let me go
But your love is killing and not healing
Because you suffocate me until death do us part

I got some things I need to get off my chest
So I can finally breathe

You wrote me a story where I finally get the leading role
Its horror and melancholy
But I triumph in the end
But it wasn't worth it
Because Pennywise still haunts me

You've sown my mouth shut
So emotion resides in the muscles of my face and the crevices of my mind
You make me want to holler when you call my name
You wretched torturous bitch
I hate you
That's why you died before me

Where do I go from here?
This path has come to an end
Do you just disappear?
Are you just gone with the wind?

Thanks for the walk in the park
But, I cannot be your friend
And I have to protect mine from you
Until your end

After all this time
Hope is the only open door left to choose
But be careful when you choose it
Cut it may very well haunt you

CH. 13: Pain

The cost of growing something out of life when you've been thrown in a field of dirt can be very expensive. I had been provided, rather blessed, with keys that can make something grow out of nothing. Instead of spreading them and sharing those seeds with other people, I instead used it all for myself which in turn cost too much. I think about what I could have done, and what if I had made one right decision. I felt I was so busy and focused, after going through so much, on making sure my cup was full that I ignored others.

I had a friend who committed suicide. At the time, I was going through a lot myself with depression and much more instances that caused that feeling to grow. I was so focused on what I was going through and trying to take care of myself that I couldn't hear the cries from around me. I became one of those people after the incident who said I didn't know, when in reality I just didn't acknowledge. After going through what I went through, I thought back to the moment and noticed all the signs that said he needed help. I constantly beat myself up about it for a long time, and it became added weight on my life that was ultimately crushing me. It costs almost nothing to check up on your friends even in the midst of your own situations. I had wished that I had used what I was dealing with as seed to help someone else grow but instead I used it to dwell on my own shortcomings in life.

I now understand why people say they feel alone even though they have many people who care about them. They mean that they are alone in the sense that they either have no one that can relate to what they are feeling, or the people that care cannot provide them what they need to make it through their hardship. At the time, I was one of those people who cared, but because of my circumstances, I was not able to provide what my friend had needed so it came at a cost.

This experience changed me forever when it comes to mental health and mental health advocacy. Because I have been through this amongst many other things, I can provide true valuable support to people who feel they have no one to relate to. In my friends name and many others, I used my experiences as an opportunity to save numerous lives and to open the gateway to healing that I too felt I did not have. And for instances where I feel like I cannot help someone, I make sure I know at least one person who can. This poem is based on the idea that some people invest in themselves and still end up falling short or victim to an ill mind. Your worth is not in what you have or what has happened to you, your worth is in what you survive.

Pain

Pain is plain
Insane
And brings change
But it's a burden on your brain

It's like trying to smell a rose in a field of garbage
Or trying to find a tear in a field of hurt
It's where you decided to pick a quarter in a field of pennies
And you were left with a dollar in a field of dirt

It's where your conscience told you, you had nothing
So you spent that dollar on a snack
When you could've bought some seeds
And now you can't get it back

Pain is where men don't cry
So your pain turns to hurt
It's where you looked at your bank
And thought "that's what I'm worth"

Some people say "it's better to cry now, so you can smile another day"
But if you're broke, depressed, and lonely, this isn't what you'd say
You looked sad and your friend asked if you were ok
But you didn't return the question, so you'll regret that one day

Then you got a call
Saying "Your friend took his life"
Realizing that pain can cost a dollar

Or pain can cost a life

But instead you thought "men don't cry"
So your pain turned to hurt
And you looked at your bank
And forgot your worth

And he acquired another dollar
But his mind got in the way
So he put a bullet near his brain
So move it out of the way

So pain can cost a dollar
Or pain can cost a life
But pain cost him both
So will you get it right?

But hey,
It's better to cry now
So you can smile another day
And if the pain doesn't get you
The dollar will find a way

Pain

CH. 14 Sweat

On the verge of doing something that you may regret, there is always hesitation that will make you sweat or think about it a little longer. Maybe this is because there is no turning back once the decision has been executed. I have felt dead on the inside until this very moment of hesitation, and suddenly I felt nothing but life.

I had a moment in time when I cried all the tears I could possibly cry, and nothing had phased me anymore. This was a moment where I had truly given up, and did not care about what happens next. I had made the conscious decision to want to end it all. I was emotionless, and I did not want to cause a ruckus. And in the moment where I was about to give myself the quick way to achieve peace, I felt something. In the midst of my long time lack of emotion, I felt something that made me hesitate. After feeling dead inside and feeling like I had cried all the tears that I could, I felt emotion. Because of this emotion, I knew that the time was not now.

This sweat dropping moment was a moment that saved my life. Although I had felt this emotion before, I was glad to have it because it meant that there was a fight that still lit bright inside of me. My hesitation meant to me that there was hope inside of me that believed there was prosperity at the end of this long journey.

The thoughts after still persisted, but I realized they were just thoughts that weren't backed up by actions. So, for this particular circumstance, I was very appreciative because my rise was inevitable.

Sweat

My hands are sweaty
So my fingers might slip
The gun is in my hand
And I'm hoping I don't slip

It's a scary world when you can't cry no more
The pain is so deep you can't see it in your eyes no more
Digging holes so deep that I can bury myself
I got a hole in my heart and it's affecting my health

I like to take things that are mine
But doesn't everyone though?
So if it's life, what's the risk?
Would anyone know?

It could be today
But tomorrow's right around the corner
And if I'm running late
Like a job, I'm a goner

They say it has to get worse before it gets better
But my hearts already cold and I can't survive this weather
The gun is on my hip and I reach inside the leather
And if my fingers were to slip, will it get better?

There's a god and there's a devil
With whom shall I dance?
I asked God cuz he seemed special
But he didn't give me a hand
All I really wanted was for him to give me a chance
The devil laughed in my face and said let's have this dance

My conscience was laughing in my face
Him and the devil, what's the difference?
I just wish that he was dead
And I wish him good riddance

I want to cry but I can't cry no more
All my tears are dry and I can't hide it no more
They say take a deep breath but I can't sigh no more
If we are all already dying can I die some more

I can't say this word of shame and word of help
Band-Aids cover my wounds and I can't heal myself
Healing takes time and my time is wealth
So if healing took it all, I have none for myself

I have so much to say
But my feelings aren't spoken
And I go through all these days
Either breaking, broke, or broken

I was asked when you grow up
Who do you want to be
I named everything I liked
But none of them was me

So let my hands sweat
And let my fingers slip
And if this shall make you triggered
Then I've already tightened the grip

CH. 15: Suicidal Thoughts

You ever wonder what it is like to have a mind that gave up? To not care about what or who hurt you so much so that you develop a ruthless mindset in dealing with your issues? Biggie smalls song "Suicidal thoughts" is the perfect representation of what that feels like, except I added my own little twist.

I came to a point where every thought became extreme. I did not care what people thought because I felt there was no one out there to help me. I felt unique in my circumstances. But the truth was that I needed to experience this so that once I made it through, other people would not feel like they are the only one experiencing what they are going through. I write poetry like this to give it life so that when I am lost in a situation, I can refer back and feel like I have someone to relate to with that someone being a past version of myself. In this sense, I gave life to my feelings via my poetry so that I will never be alone in the future obstacles I may encounter.

I have encountered people who put me down in my lowest moments. These people I refer to as peasants. They wanted to seem perfect and bring discredit to my struggles, so I gave a reality check to show exactly what it is like to stand in my shoes. And what do you know?! They couldn't even stand for a day in what I stood in for a lifetime. My scars show and tell stories, but I wear mine with pride because it shows I've survived 100% of my worst days. But to keep them hidden from the world and to portray a problem free life highlights your weakness.

I am not one who lives in fear of the thought of whether or not I am going to hell. I could honestly care less.

But I know that I live in my truth every day I breathe, and accept myself for who I am. Enjoy this suicidal thought.

Suicidal Thoughts

When I die fuck it I want to go to hell
Cuz I'm a piece of shit it aint hard to fucking tell
Don't make sense going to heaven with the goodie goodies
Dressed in white, I like black tims and black hoodies

But I can tell hell lives in my head
And I tell hell I am going to bed
And if you shall take me in my sleep, this will be the sweetest song I ever said
But if not, this note will be the longest thought I ever read

You only cry for help when you believe there's help to cry for
You only live in purpose if you believe there's something to die for
Or these thoughts give you a life to lie for
Until these suicidal thoughts become actions you die for

I can't explain the pain that lingers in my brain
When my thoughts go insane and I can't tame
The name that my thoughts give fame
Until it shames my life and makes my fate plain

I can't live like this, so I die like this
Or I can write like this
To reminisce about the pain
Until my pen is pissed

But my thoughts make my pen lethal
And if suicide was already written then this will be the sequel
And if I make you think about death then my pen should be illegal

Because if suicidal thoughts are the devil then bring rise to the spirit of evil

Now to the people who want to be peaceful
There's always fecal inside the steeple
Shitty on the inside
And on the out it looks regal

So, let's air things out

Your one, not many
Your weak, your feeble
That's why we live in chaos
So, we can rest peaceful

And If you think your peaceful
Let me hand you a needle
So, you can take your life
And see that death will be equal

Cover your body in diesel
To set fire to the pain
Then put you in a cathedral
So, your pain can fill people

If you think, there's peace in life
Then your thoughts are being deceitful
But don't let this pen control you
Because this fecal is lethal

Here's a warning

When trouble comes

it will appear as if he's see-through
He has a pen like mine
But his is legal

If you see him across the street,
Then let the horse out of the steeple
He has a match just for you,
Because you've covered yourself in diesel to be peaceful

My ink needs a refill

When life lessens, you need life lessons to keep you alive
But we are all dying just to make a living
So, what's the point of living
If we're just dying just to make livings

I die in time and I live in moments
But my life is a moment that has lasted too long
Guilt never exists in a mind that resists the urge to live
Because we're only cutting ourselves off with the scissors
you've provided

The ones who live in peace always die in chaos
But the ones who live in chaos always die in peace
Whether it's hell or heaven we end the same way
But heaven created hell, so it's the same either way

So, When I die fuck it I want to go to hell
Cuz I'm a piece of shit it aint hard to fucking tell
Don't make sense going to heaven with the goodie goodies
Dressed in white, I like black tims and black hoodies

But this is just a suicidal thought

CH. 16 One Chance

One chance. A feeling that you have one last time before you succumb to the obstacles that your mind had been struggling with. A lot of the times I had felt very close to prosperity, but I was far from reality. Why would I give up now when I had come so far and have been through so much? Well, maybe that's because I did not know how much further I had to go. Broken and defeated, I felt as if I had nothing left but this "terrible" life I was living. But I decided to give it one last chance to keep fighting this seemingly everlasting battle with myself.

I was one who was crushed. But I interpreted a new essential meaning to being crushed. You have to fold the dough before it rises. You have to crush the grapes before it turns into wine. You have to apply heat and pressure to a wrinkled shirt before its ironed. I learned that crushing was a stage, not a destination. I learned that I had to be crushed in order to step into my true potential. It is imperative that we are all crushed at some point in life so that when we experience something that seems to be defeating us, we don't die.

Fighting for our inner peace will never be peaceful. We cannot live in fear because when we are on our way to our destination, we will use that fear as a stop sign. More often than not, many of us have one chance to get things right, and we're not going out without a fight.

One Chance

Riveting inside my head
These thoughts slowly become real life
I saw the danger sign by the playground
And I decided to have a little fun

The thought that fought hard for acceptance
Here is a letter of assurance

Dear Thoughts,

When waves became tsunamis
It was like you washed me away
And as I searched for a place to escape
I found poetry as a place to hide

I tried to rise up but you said "get down! There's a storm coming"
But when I had gotten down,
I couldn't get back up
You held me down and I was stuck

This was the moment you introduced me to someone named depression
He seemed nice at first but the melancholy was unbearable
That was when I met anxiety
And I hated that bitch

I slowly became gloomy yet angry
I craved happiness and peace daily
So much so that the most dangerous thought I've ever had was created

“I’d do anything for peace, even if I have to kill myself”

The world wouldn’t understand because we are all too human
If death is just a part of life, why does everyone run from it
I have nothing to lose, so I choose to run towards it

Tragedy and silence have the exact same voice
Life is all I got and heaven is all in my brain
Whispering “Come to me”
But my left hemisphere says “Hell naw”

I shall call this the battle of the thoughts
Where there is only one entrance and one exit
One mic and one knife
And one chance

CH. 17: Me

A sense of self-realization will help one see the truth of whom we are and assist in becoming aware of our experiences or circumstances. Knowing and accepting my circumstances that fueled the decline of my mental health was the first step in healing. I needed to do this in order to become successful in my future endeavors.

I had to become willing to say that I am a person who is broken. For a long time, I was in denial. It came to a point where I had no choice but to truly show who I am with all my flaws because the things that I bottled up inside me for so long had begun to expose themselves. This was the first experience in learning who I am. I went through life acknowledging everyone. We can see everyone in a room except ourselves; that's why we have mirrors. It was time to see myself for who I was. It was time to face the mirror that tells no lies.

While looking in this mirror, I had begun acknowledging all my flaws that I have ignored for so long. I looked closely at every imperfection. I began speaking my cold-hearted truth, and then asked myself what are you going to do about it. I knew it didn't matter what the truth was, but it mattered how can I make my truth benefit me. While in my lowest point of this deep analysis of myself, I realized that some things are only imperfections if we believe them to be as such. Once I realized this, I was able to accept myself for who I was, and step into my destiny to succeed.

Me

There was a king who was cursed
His life got only worse
His mind had dispersed
So he put his heart first

But then it broke

And the king had almost croaked
On his conscience, he had choked
He ended his life in a note

He was crying inside
Felt dead but was alive
You could see it in his eyes
Because he didn't want them open
They were red and soaking
His mind
Broken
His heart
Broken
On his life, he was choking

He was cut deep
Because every day he would weep
He was fighting in his sleep
And thought his life was so cheap

It cut like a blade
His life was in the shade
All he wanted was to fade
Because his mind was in a cave

And so the blade was to his wrist
The blade was to his wrist!
He knew the time had come when his mind couldn't resist
But he fought
And he shook
But his soul
He had took
From enemies
To memories
To leave behind his legacy
His melody rose heavily
As violins played steadily
His second thought was destiny
But secretly a parody
The great escape tastes heavenly
Because his mind would sleep so restfully
How would he know this day would come if he fought his mind so helplessly
But he,
Felt heated and defeated
So he,
Used his burn and succeeded
Cuz he,
Knew his heart through his weakness
And he,

Was me

Phase 3:

The Lost Ones (Broken Friendships)

CH. 18: Dance

Be careful of the "friends" who tempt you with your own desires that lead to your demise. The ill intentions of people are oftentimes hidden or disguised by friendships. Most friendships aren't friendships, they are just people who have the convenience of proximity. Just because someone is around you all the time, does not mean that person is your friend. Oftentimes, people use the friend term too loosely. They think that just because someone says "Hi" with a smile, then that means this person is a nice person. I have learned to be careful with these types of judgements because most people are mainly looking to level up in life even if it is at your expense.

Some people use people for what they are worth and then leave them hanging. A friendship can be a prison sentence, but most people only know that after being released. Additionally, some people don't have enough courage to end a "friendship" because they have known the person for years. They have created emotional ties that have become too thick to cut. We have to learn that the term colleague and friend are not words meant to be used interchangeably. Although we must make our own judgements, we have to acknowledge repeated patterns and behaviors. Too often we expect something different from someone who has not known us different behaviors. Because I am an observant person, I have observed people get walked on by other perceived friends and was able to avoid dancing with the devil.

Don't dance with the devil and end up in hell.

Dance

Everyone's a friend until you drop the r
They are always pleasant until you drop the l
First they love you then they switch
Like from a star to rats
And all it takes is one letter
For them to switch back

Take you to a party
But careful when you dance with
The devil
Is hidden in a sentence
After the ending of life

It may last forever
Or maybe a minute or two
But a minute is in a sentence
That doesn't end with you
Making it hard to period
Without a question of time

People say "what?! He's an angel!"
But so was the devil
You were dancing with him at the party
While his friends without the r was looking for a shovel

He was hidden behind his moves
Dancing with a girl named Bee
But Bee was too blind to see
So she D I E Deed
So her friends without the R
Doesn't dance with the devil

In a sentence

CH. 19 Lash Out

An anger riveting inside of me caused a ruthlessness of thoughts with no mercy, so much so, that I lashed out leaving people who this poem would normally offend speechless. The anger that was sparked inside of me does not care about feelings or aftermath. It does not care about who's hurt or what gets damaged in the process of my lashing out. Some people cannot be pushed to their anger limit because what arises as a result could be too detrimental to the person or entity on the receiving end.

I am not responsible for other people's feelings because it is up to you whether I get to control them or not. I was a person that once you've crossed me or someone I care about, then I become emotionally detached. I no longer care about what you feel or how you feel. I am neither empathetic nor sympathetic because what you did was so wrong that I couldn't see what sane human being could do something so vile. This story that I am about to tell is one that speaks the truth. If one shall say that I am brutally honest, then I should return the question that if the truth is able to be brutal, why did you give me the opportunity to speak it?

This story centers around a person who brings someone down for her own benefit, and lacked the courage to stand up for what was right even if it meant that she would be subject to her own detriment. The situation that she created to protect herself from embarrassment is absolutely disgusting. One can only assume that this was done due to her own insecurity, selfishness, and lies. As she was caught one time after spreading her legs every weekend, she couldn't fathom the thoughts that people would create in their own minds so instead of taking accountability, she folded. She sought asylum via sympathy. But despite what circumstances resulted, she didn't receive it. Instead, she lived out her days lying in her own guilt by her own drunk admissions. I guess her plan b didn't work this time. Even her mother conjured up a story to try to save her, but that only pointed out how much of a flower she was that stemmed from dead roots. This meant that her failure was inevitable from the very beginning. A guilty conscience can sometimes be fatal as proven by her attempted actions.

This was a case where the truth hurt so bad that she tried to bury it. But she was not careful about the dirt she threw at other peoples feet, because it ended up being the same dirt that she was almost buried with. I live in a world where faith is my shield, and truth is my sword; the truth can kill. Some people lash out with the truth, while the others become victims of their own lies.

Lash Out

Prep yourself for what's to come
Because when a king gets angry
The voices go numb
Careful in these streets you're about to walk upon
Because all this pain and anger will run you over
And keep driving on

I got some things to get off my chest
Because what used to sit well can't sit well
I realize this life is full of fake people and opportunists
So let me expose the new guests on my list of peasants
In which they will become the lowest of them all
For the peasantry they let run amuck in my kingdom

It is a privilege, in their case, to be called a peasant
Because although they are one of the lowest in the ranking structure
They are still one step above the roaches
Barely...
But as I go on
A demotion keeps screaming in my ear
"Let the roaches scatter"

An anger is riveting inside of me
Because I can't understand how a peasant can lie
So much
Because I can't understand how a peasant can be insecure
So much
Because I can't understand how a peasant can be selfish
So much

Because I can't understand how a peasant can buss it wide open to an entire fleet
And STILL won't feel ran through
This is me saying no offense,
But all offense
Make sense?

She said her cat wet but it's dry to every other platoon
Asbestos everywhere because people keep knocking down her walls
In her house in the slums
Busted it open for groceries so she can get some clout
Oh how we stan a standard-less peasant
A fraudulent peasant
A plan B type of peasant
A type of peasant looking for sympathy points
Well peasant be gone

Let me define a peasant once again for those in the back
Refer to The Great Escape: Thinking the Thoughts Away Page 123-125
The definition of a peasant
"They who wish to rise upon your fall"
There's a lot of that going on today in the kingdom

Oh how regret can make a peasant do the craziest of things
She was a flower who grew from dead roots
Mother included
BUT FLOWERS CAN'T SURVIVE WITH DEAD ROOTS
That's why she broken now
Now watch her die slow

But what goes around comes around

And just like how she robbed someone
I shall do the same
How about I put my pistol in her mouth and tell her "Suck it!"
But she better watch her head because it bust though
The last thing she'll see is death
Staring her in her eye's
Just like the hills do
And look death in the face
And he'll wink

Watch as I lash
And crash
And bash
The person who's in sync with the above
The dirt you throw at people's feet will be the same dirt you're buried with
This is the day where "God don't like ugly"
And you're hideous
But if God shall wish you to stay upon this earth
I pray Satan draws you into the depths of hell with your dead roots
But if I'm lucky
This would be the day God and Satan shall come together
For the taking down of a peasant with no standards
Because it's time to lash out
To get the ash out

CH. 20 Clout

When people go out of their way to diminish what you are trying to accomplish is how you know that you are stepping into your destiny. A lot of the time a hater is someone who envies you. They want what you have but do not have a means to get it. So as a result, they attempt to bring you down so they can have company at the bottom where they are used to residing at. But, when we refuse to stoop to those levels of peasantry, they laugh when we stumble or fall along our life journey. But it is sad that they don't realize that at my lowest, I am still higher than them.

When you have a lot of influence, a lot of people will do any and everything to gain some type of power or influence for themselves at your expense. People want what you have without knowing the struggle you had to go through to get it. In this sense, they want the benefit of seeing a rainbow without having to go through the storm. Having clout breeds jealousy, but it is expected from people who are dissatisfied with their position in life.

People will be upset that you were brought up with a silver spoon just because they were brought up with plastic forks and paper plates. What some don't realize is that a lot of people who have this silver spoon, had to cope with plastic forks before they could get into the position they are in now. Although many people are disproportionately disadvantaged in this world, many are stuck in that mentality that keeps them in that position. Sometimes when people feel that they are in this inferior position for so long, there is a hatred that builds up for people who are seen as elite compared to them. They wonder why not me, instead of asking how. Oftentimes, haters attempt to get the easy way out of many things and get mad when someone else achieves the very same thing they struggled doing. Then, in an attempt to bring someone down, they try to bring discredit on your achievements. People don't talk about people who lose, they talk about people who win. Being hateful towards someone unwarrantedly means that person has already won. Haters lose once again.

Clout

A hater here
A hater there
Always plotting
But I don't care
You cross me once
You cross me twice
You kindly crumble
Because I'm precisely nice

They know I'm a poet
And they have no clout
They were watching my moves
So I saw how it played out
When I tripped, they smiled
When I stumbled, they yelled
When I fouled, they applauded
When I ran, they trailed
Trying to watch from the sky to see me fail
Cuz I shine all day and into the night
So they tried to fly to see me fail
But kings don't crumble so you missed your flight

A hater here
A hater there
Always plotting
But I don't care
You cross me once
You cross me twice
You kindly crumble
Because I'm precisely nice

Go against me

Then you made a mistake
If you don't believe me
Just ask all my rivals
If I had known you were plotting
I would've laced your steak
But kings don't kill
So that means you're suicidal
They want me to help them
But I'm no magician
Until it comes to a fight
Then I'm a mortician
I don't get physical
But I do get lyrical
Cuz I rebuke your presence
Now that's biblical
Now I'm killing your conscience
And you don't know what to do
So now you're starting to scramble
And you're looking for clues
You can't stand against me
So what do you do?
Stand with me, but guess what?
I don't stand next to you

A hater here
A hater there
Always plotting
But I don't care
You cross me once
You cross me twice
You kindly crumble
Because I'm precisely nice

They told me I would lose
But I won
They said I didn't make them
So I "sonned"
I flip them like a patty
Then I run
And now they can't catch up
That's a pun

You see how I'm twisting this rhyme
Like I'm twisting a lime
With a sour taste in your mouth
And now you're twisting through time
They said I was toxic
And I was wasting their time
But now they are struggling
And they sniffing some lines
Roaming through the streets
Karma killing their time
While I'm sitting here classy
I'm just sipping my wine

A hater here
A hater there
Always plotting
But I don't care
You cross me once
You cross me twice
You kindly crumble
Because I'm precisely nice

I'm no mathematician
But if my calculations are correct

A hater plus a peasant
Equals a hating ass peasant
Your mind will never match my type of intellect
Cuz checking a peasant is a kings' tradition
Now, If you multiply your value with anything else
You would, no matter what, always get zero
Now if you want to check my work
Then, you should check yourself
Cuz if you check a peasant
You'll be your own hero

A hater here
A hater there
Always plotting
But I don't care
You cross me once
You cross me twice
You kindly crumble
Because I'm precisely nice

I can tell you're getting flustered
Maybe even a bit angry
Cuz your soft, you're custard
And you're getting a bit hangry
See now I'm winning
So I say aha!
Remember the beginning
You do? Ha-ha
Since in the beginning
You wanted me to fail
But now it's too late
And your ship has sailed
They dissed me

And wanted to take the same route
Then missed me
And with the wind you uproot
Wanting to watch me fail
So you're up in the sky
Watching me succeed
But hey, you tried
But in this game
There are no A's
There's F's for effort
And shoulder chips like lays

A hater here
A hater there
Always plotting
But I don't care
You cross me once
You cross me twice
You kindly crumble
Because I'm precisely nice

You are the enemy
So you're no friend of me
But if you were in the past
Then you are a frenemy
You see yourself as 20
But you'll never be 10 of me
Not even a whole
Not even a tenth of me
You will never compare
Not never not ever
Cuz you got no clout
And never will, not ever

See this was a lesson
And you always missed class
But if I take out the first two letters
Then maybe I'll see you in class

CH 21: Mercy

This is one of those times when people say "when someone shows you who they are, believe them the first time". I am one who does not like to judge a person solely based on what other people think, however, if I did it would save my time from being wasted. This friendship at the time was one that I had to kill, but the worst thing about it is that I didn't have to kill it with my own words. I killed it with the words of other people who had the same or similar interactions, and most importantly, the person's own words. I did not go out of my way to put someone down because I did not have to.

This friend at the time had many enemies who used to say the most disheartening things, but I have always felt they were misunderstood. They did not know this person to the extent that I did. Although we had a moment we're we had fallen out as friends, I was never the type of person to unite with a former friend's enemies for the sole purpose of bringing someone down. That is peasant behavior. Sometimes, it is best to let someone know how you've perceived them so that they are self-aware.

When you truly care about someone, sometimes you have to care enough to let them go. Oftentimes, things that we experience have to be learned by ourselves in order to understand the true lesson behind each circumstance. In order to see improvement, one has to be willing to recognize their own faults and to listen to the voices that surround them. This sense of self-awareness is healthy for providing personal growth in life.

More importantly, with this friendship, I knew that with all the anger I had inside of me, I had to not act out of anger. I knew based on previous circumstances in my life that I did not have to react because the spirit of karma always does her due diligence. Many times, people have to be knocked down off their feet in order to re-evaluate their life journey thus far to ensure that the right path is being taken. As a friend, it is important to not have mercy when it comes to allowing one to learn from their own behaviors. Oftentimes, the burden that some people bestow upon others have to be felt by their own conscience in order for them to understand the magnitude of the weight that other people accept due to their own short-comings. In the end, wish them the best and move on, or else you too may become victim of the same circumstance.

Mercy

Are you his puppet?
He is selfish
He can't even help himself
Don't waste your time
He isn't gone yet
Yo, fuck him dude
He doesn't give a shit
If it was anyone else, would they still be here
Why is he still here? He should just leave
He is using you
He's fucked up
Nobody should ever beef with Gibbs
Wow, I can't believe he did that
Fuck him, he's so selfish
He's so stupid
He's a fucking idiot
He doesn't deserve to be here
He's just a spoiled rich kid
He was spoon-fed everything
So ungrateful

Sniffing lines that aren't meant to be crossed
Breaking bonds that aren't meant to be made
Killing time that wasn't meant to be wasted
Beneath that of peasantry, and lying with the roaches
He was the devil
Words from thine own mouth

Wanting war
It's just begun
You picked me wrong

I’ve already won
Kill his conscience with NO MERCY
Karma works in my favor
Good Luck

CH. 22: Predator

Never in my life have I ever met someone so evil and disgusting. All the warning signs were there but unfortunately I like to give people a benefit of doubt. I had been warned and warned but I tried to only focus on the good in this thing. I use "thing" because I would not dare to call something who is a monster, roach, and inhumane, a person. I was done so wrong, but unfortunately for them, I am God's child. And he showed this diabolical roach and anyone who was working against me that I am protected from any form of demonic evil that attempts to rise from the deepest pits of hell in order to take me down. They failed to realize in this attempt that I had already been crowned king of my life and there was nothing that breathed the same air as I did that would stand against my destiny to rise through every occasion.

The lies and deceit caused this predator to falter. The only thing that I had that was working for me was my faith and my truth, and that was all I needed. Brace yourselves for the story that is about to arise, but it is time for the truth to surface. The name of this individual whose character I absolutely despise with every fiber of my being is John Smoke. This waste of skin of an individual made an attempt to smear my name and character with lies and deceit in an attempt to protect himself. There was a drunken night where I was with John, and I had woken up the next morning feeling as if something bad happened to me. The alcohol that I had drank the night prior fogged my memory, but the feelings of the morning after when I looked at my sheets and went to the bathroom was very telling. It left me to question what exactly happened to me because I had a suspicion that I had been victimized due to a potential particular circumstance that happened the night before. In an attempt to find out after feeling the way I did when I woke up, I questioned him about what happened the night before. He looked at me out the corner of his eye and walked away very suspiciously as if he knew what I was referring to. A couple days passed by and during those couple days I gave him the opportunity to talk, but I never got a response. Next thing you know, I am being called into an office to be informed that I have been accused of sexual assault. This was mind-boggling because it told me everything that I needed to know of what my suspicions were of what could've happened to me that night. Particularly, the sheets and the bathroom incident that I had the morning after were implanted in my mind forever from that point forward.

For obvious reasons, I believed that John Smoke knowingly accused me of such action because he was fearful that he would be on the receiving end of the troubling circumstances that would arise if I were to report him for the same. Because of this deception that he created, I was looked at as the potential bad guy in this situation. As a result, I was investigated in which a prosecution lawyer was actively trying to conjure up any potential evidence that he could use against me. The prosecution lawyer wrote a statement saying that there was probable cause for the allegation against me. He had built an entire case, and during this time I was not able to tell my side of the story because of the lack of representation due to the schedule of the one defense lawyer available to this organization. Once I was able to meet with the person who was going to be representing me, I detailed to him everything I knew from that night and the morning after in which he helped me file a report against John Smoke. I provided all my evidence to include the sheets to the appropriate authorities. The agent in which I gave the evidence had shown blatant disregard of the allegation I was making by laughing over the phone at my situation in his office to his colleagues. In addition, he tried to tell my lawyer that he was not allowed to be in the room while I gave a statement. Little did I know, making a report on my own behalf was a waste of time. This is because the same prosecution lawyer that already built a case against me and was actively trying to prosecute me, was the same lawyer that determined that there was no probable cause for the allegation that I was making. Some would call this being corrupt or a conflict of interest.

Throughout this whole process I had lost many friends and acquaintances that judged me based on what they heard without ever having to hear my story. As the process progressed, it was shown that there were videos of the alleged area in which John accused me of sexual assault. None of those videos confirmed any of the allegations that was brought against me. In fact, a lot of the evidence highlighted a lot of the many lies that John tried to tell in order to protect himself. Furthermore, he tried to get his fiancé, who was cheating on him according to John, to give a statement against me even though he was not there for the incident. In fact, his fiancé lied and said he knew me very well, had classes together, and made up a conversation saying I confided in him for things, and even was deceptive about his current location when giving a statement over the phone.

However, as I said in the beginning, all I had was my truth and God and that was all I needed. John has been accused of sexual assault and harassment multiple times in the past in which I had been warned of. The agent who was laughing at my allegation ended up dying randomly in this process. The prosecution lawyer who was corrupt left the organization that year and made a fool of himself when presenting all of his flimsy and contradictory evidence to the powers that be. And I was found innocent in every aspect of this investigation and was able to move on with my life. But let's not forget that my allegation was never taken seriously and was thrown out because of the blatant disregard by the prosecution lawyer.

Thankfully, in my case, the lies never had a chance to stand against the truth. Although the system was against me, I had my faith and was protected by God. After this incident, someone told me that John ended up falling victim to his own repeated stupid decisions and was accused of the same thing in a similar situation with someone else. I was also informed by what I would call a credible source that he had multiple allegations against him for sexual harassment. I find this funny because when I made an allegation, none of it was taken seriously.

After my innocence was determined, I was given a document that said this situation will be disposed without prejudice. In an attempt for John to look less ignorant, he started an entire campaign called Speak Up out of spite on Go Fund Me in an attempt to initially raise $500,000 to ambiguously give voices to victims of sexual assault. In my opinion, to use this false incident that he conjured up to possibly profit off other people's pain especially with him being someone who's been accused of sexual assault and harassment a thousand times is absolutely diabolical.

The mental agony that this entire situation had caused me to be what would be traumatizing to most people. This unfortunate situation revealed some people's true character, and severed a lot of relationships that needed to be ended. However, let's make one thing clear. While people made campaigns to spite me, they failed to realize that the loudest voices are not always the strongest. The fiercest of storms come from the calmest seas. I am an ocean leaping wide, and while you were building a ship to conquer my seas, it sank miserably. You can't preach for the voiceless when you don't have one yourself. A lie can never stand against the truth. Standing on the backs of people who are actually negatively affected by certain issues so that you can feel better about your lies is disgusting, pure peasantry, and predatory behavior. Let your enemies convince themselves of their lies, and they will forever be a running joke. Because even though they worked night and day to take you down, ran campaigns to spite you and profit off their lies, and tried to convince people of their lies to take their side in order to lead a rebellion against you; you rose through the occasion. This just goes to show that the truth always hurts.

P.S. In case of a rebuttal, I have all the receipts (evidence) to corroborate everything that was said above.

Predator

I should've listened when they warned me
I should have clipped you when they said you were a worn leaf
Be careful about a smile with the worn teeth
Because I gave it a chance and now it's on me

Now I'm losing sleep and I can barely eat
I fake smile because I got to get through the week
It's like you put a tare inside my masterpiece
The cut is small, but the pain is deep

The pain wreaks
The pain sneaks
I was strong but now the tough's weak on a tough week having tough sleep

My head hangs below my chest
Wishing death with every breath
Wanting to go right but everything's left
Portraying me as the thief but you committed the theft

Now I'm the monster
I'm the horrible person
My friends turned their backs
Now I question is life worth it

Your life is full of lies
Where side eyes turn to sly eyes
Smiles in the face but the eyes cry
It's a tough world when the lies lie

A predator in disguise
Where your pain is so deep that you must give some of it away
Choosing me as the victim
But your disguise tells lies

Night terrors of that day
The day my dignity went astray
The day my sanity went away
The day you stole my life as pay

For your debts!
This non-refundable transaction
That I will regret every waking day
Even words can't express what I want to say

I wake every morning and I remember the pain
The pain you bestowed upon me as I lay helpless
The euphoria made my pain plain
And made your brain selfish

As blood smears on toilet rolls
And stains the water
The piercing pain raising questions
Causing a dull moment that lasts a lifetime

I want to yell my story at the top of Mt. Everest
But nothing will come out
Because predators protect their selfish
And a counter causes doubt

I should've listened when they warned me

I should have clipped you when they said you were a worn leaf
Be careful about a smile with the worn teeth
Because I gave it a chance and now it’s on me

Predator

CH. 23: Crumble

I am one of God's children because I have made it through everything that came to destroy me. I learned quickly that I shall not seek vengeance towards people who sought to see me fail. Romans 12:19 says "Beloved, never avenge yourselves, but leave it to the wrath of God, for it is written, 'Vengeance is mine, I will repay,' says the Lord". Although when the opportunity to have vengeance was readily available, I did not act. Instead, I stood by and watched with high emotions even though I wanted to teach someone a lesson. It wasn't until later when I realized that this "lesson" was not mine to teach.

Imagine a bridge that has many pillars, but it is one pillar that if knocked, the whole bridge would come crashing down. Essentially, I knew that I was this one pillar that was holding everything together for this person. I've seen all types of people cross this bridge, and I could've easily caused turmoil. However, this bridge was bound to fall one day anyway because the foundation was not strong enough to hold the weight that this bridge carried. God essentially tapped me (the pillar) and told me to step back. And as I stepped back, the whole bridge went falling.

I was the support that kept this former friend intact. I was taken advantage of and used because this person did not know how to support their own life. I was treated like a stray dog in the street, so it was inevitable that one day I will have to take a step back. And when I did, the truth of everything going on in this person's life showed as everything crumbled into pieces. And instead of helping this person pick up the pieces, I realized that it was best for them to do it by themselves.

From this point forward, I refuse to carry the weight of someone else's burden because I've got my own to worry about. I could've broken my back trying to help you, but then I would not be able to care for myself. How foolish of me. I learned that there will be people who will try to kill you, defeat you, or humiliate you as a weapon in an attempt on your life. I saw those weapons and remembered that God said no weapons formed against me shall prosper. I have prevailed in these instances every time, and have been able to watch God protect me from things that he did not send. The book of psalms says that "May those who try to kill me be defeated and confused. May those who are happy because of my troubles be turned back and disgraced. May those who make fun of me be dismayed by their defeat." All in all, people will read a thousand books on how to take you down, but fails to realize that you are one who writes them. And unfortunately for their own sake, that is just the way the cookie crumbles.

Crumble

I hope you carry your crumbs with pride
Because when you tried to go against the grain
You broke into pieces
And I watched you crumble

I cannot believe I let a worthless roach with back acne touch my crown
Ew!!
You and your crumbs can crawl back into your hole
Because my size 15 has no mercy

There is a distinct difference between me and you
I'm a poet, author, and entrepreneur
You're a peasant, a drunk, who smells like a sewer
We don't compare

Carry your crumbs and walk your sorry path with your peasant boots
Because you will never be able to fit in my shoes
Just like a cookie
You crumble with every bite

Notice how as soon as I stepped away everything went crashing
And all you have left of your cookie is a bunch of crumbs
You prayed I would fall and vanish into thin air
But that's not the way the cookie crumbles

The deceit and the lies you tried to spread across your cookie
And little did you know, the pressure made you break
A wise man never reads books, he writes them

But roaches can never understand this type of intellect

Carry your crumbs to feed to your fellow roaches
But watch how I step because you may get stomped
You're just like a cookie
Crumbling

CH. 24

Peasantry on a Boat

All aboard
Let's catch this ride
Evan, Marquis, Jack, and I
Tristan and Racheal
Wish I had a date too
Cuz Nick was no saint
And it was only day 2

But wait there's more
There's just one more
A fiend? A peasant? A joke? A whore?
Or could it be all four?
And he was no Mike
But the last name was the same
And he was high as a kite
But dumb as a brick
Peasantry

At its highest peak
The wolf would howl
And the dog would leak
This animal was foul
Only dreamt of getting it on
Cuz there was no humping
If you had a pig with a blanket
It was nothing but funny
A joke is what I'd call it
But hey, peasant tried

And failed every time
And sniffed every line
And committed every crime
And got every fine
But a peasant got to do, what a peasant got to do

But then came a turn
Within an inch of his life!!
His bags were packed
And he found his flight
Lost as a puppy
But dumb as a log
Cuz this peasant was rocking in white
All night long

Peasantry on a Boat

CH. 25: Trust

I am at a point in my life where trusting someone is a feeling of vulnerability. With trust, I became susceptible to all potential wounds. Maybe this is because I was broken, or maybe it is because I was hurt in the past. But either way, trust is something that I do not want to have a lot of at this point in my life. I guess trauma really does that to you.

In order to effectively utilize trust, you must first have to learn how to trust yourself. I had to learn how to trust myself to step back when it was time to step back, and let go when it was time to let go. I had to believe in my ability to not let myself get hurt. I have been hurt many times, and trust was a pain that I could not fathom.

Oftentimes, trust is used as a weapon to invoke deception for one's own personal gain. The level of trust you have for a person can very well be the depth of your wound that results. At first glance, you never know someone's intentions, but if you have been around the block a few times, you begin to notice the signs. I've learned that when it comes to people having the choice to choose between me or you, based on your expectations, you will be disappointed every time.

A person who is trying to deceive you will do everything in their power to make sure their intentions are not compromised. They will take extra steps to make sure that even though they are broken, they show all the better parts of them. These are people who may want to bring you down just so they can have someone to relate to.

The only person I trust at the end of the day is myself because I always know my own intentions, and how I act in certain situations. I learned to become self-reliant for many aspects of my life, so I do not have to trust or depend on other people and end up disappointed. I know that if I have short-comings then it is because of my own ability, and not someone else's who may have been trying to sabotage me the entire time.

Trust

Trust is the worst pain I have ever experienced
A disgusting human instinct
It's like an itch that won't go away
Trust hurts

It feels like you got shot without getting shot
But you stay alive to suffer from the wounds
It's that "it was either me or you" mindset
And that "I choose me" decision
that makes you take a knife and stab the person that helped you get there
Trust hurts

It's a place where everyone wears the mask
So, you don't know who's who
Its where actors are acting
And ghosts don't boo

It's where the broken are laughing
And the liars are crying
Or the criers are laughing
Or the broken are lying
Trust hurts

Trust is a demon carrying its most deadly equipment
that greets its blind victim with much eager before he's killed
Trust is the that one friend that sleeps with your girl or your man
while you're dating them
Trust is nothing but a feeling of vulnerability
Trust hurts

CH. 26: Rest in Peace

You can't help people who do not take the necessary steps to help themselves. This was a situation that I was faced with that caused me to lose myself in the process of helping someone else. After numerous attempts to help the broken break less, there is only so much fixing one can do before you start inheriting the wounds in which they are trying to fix.

Because of this, I had to learn how to let go. However, letting go felt like I knew I would be killing this individual in doing so. My support was the only thing keeping this friend alive which was the reason I kept trying to hold on. But the wounds started to transfer to me and affect my life, so I had to let go. I knew that the inevitable would happen, so in letting go, I felt like I was killing this person. They say hurt people hurt people, but I reckon that hurt people hurt themselves even more.

I felt guilty for having to give up on this individual, but this person was too far to reach. A flower without roots has a death that is inevitable. Friends turn into fiends, and in some instances pleasant turns into peasants. Some people will fiend for something from you that you cannot give them. And when you tell them that you can't give them what they are asking, they make you feel bad in which they begin to act within the realms of peasantry.

If you lose yourself fighting for lost causes, then you've become a part of that lost cause.

Rest in Peace

At first, I was blinded
At next, I was astonished
Third, I was skeptical
And at last, I'm reminded

You lose yourself fighting for lost causes

As I lay you to rest
I'm burying you alive
You got my best
But I got your lies
I know you're hurt
So, I'm watching you die
Now rest in peace
Farewell,
Goodbye

With every deep breath
My hearts beats slower
But letting it go will help it beat faster

I'm begging heaven please
Don't give hell to me
I see darkness approaching your corner
But you're too far to reach now
I see death in your ear
And I was supposed to be your saving grace
But not this time
Here's a rose for life
But it's cut with no roots
Rest in peace

As I lay you to rest
I'm burying you alive
You got my best
But I got your lies
I know you're hurt
So, I'm watching you die
Now rest in peace
Farewell,
Goodbye

You were my friend until you got rid of the R
you were pleasant until you got rid of the L
I used to like to dance
But not anymore
Because a dance with the devil will send me to hell

Once and for all
You're a dead man walking
A dead thought talking
A dead man

You're killing yourself
But I feel like I'm killing you
By letting you go
But my saving grace can't help you no more

I'm burying you alive
I'm watching you die
Now rest in peace
Farwell,
Goodbye

CH. 27: Forgiveness

How do you deal with all that pain that lingers on your mind, especially the pain that someone else causes you? It's like you're trapped in a prison, and the person who betrayed you has the key. Although forgiveness is sometimes for other people, at all times it should at least be for yourself.

A wise one once said "bitterness is like a cancer, it eats upon the host." Unless you are able to bear true forgiveness within your heart, then someone else's actions will always defeat you every moment you allow it to. Some bridges need to be burnt because some of us are too easily accessible.

Forgiveness

Call me and beg for forgiveness
And you shall look pathetic
I am the beholder of your freedom
The homeless man with a New York City Penthouse
I feel your sorrow because you are sorry
A sorry ass excuse that is
But I forgive you for me
Because I am free
I'm finally free

I was once a prisoner of my conscience
For a hot second that is
But tables turn like door knobs
Because what goes around, comes around
Cuz in *The Great Escape*, Karma was a bitch

Forgiveness?
Your happiness depends on it.

There is no such thing as prison in my mind
Because I am free
I am finally free

I've won the battle and war

Burn the Bridges
I have done so already
Forgive me
But only if it shall set me free
Who doesn't like free stuff?
I don't

Freedom is something that was once stolen from me

Why is it that when someone hurts you,
You're the one put in the shackles
Why is it that when someone steals my freedom
I'm the one that has to suffer
But that's a future me answer
Because I am free
I am finally free

Forgiveness isn't something you give to someone who hurt you
Forgiveness is something you give to yourself.
Staying angry steals our happiness
Cuz peasant I'm free
I'm finally free

Phase 4:

The Optimist

CH. 28: The Crown

Uneasy lies the head that wears the crown. The crown is heavy which is why only the strongest can wear it. The crown is for people who accept that they are ruler of their own life. Peasants were throwing stones at me not knowing that I was using them to build my castle.

The Crown

My rock, my heart, my success
The representation of power and legitimacy
Victory and honor
Righteousness and resurrection
Glory and immortality
One that shall not tilt with peasantry

I am king because I have a crown
I have a crown because I am the ruler of my own life
I overcame, excelled, and triumphed
I hurdled the thoughts that were running my mind
Because of resilience, hope, and faith
I have a crown because I am king

I bow to no one
Except those who have control over me
In my land, there are no such things as monarchs
But there is such thing as monarch
For when they hate the taste of my success
They mistake me for a butterfly

When they said there was no way
I pointed in a direction and said that way
When they said you'll fail
I said you're right
Forthcoming **A**n **I**mpeccable **L**ife
When they said impossible
I broke…
And said I'm possible

You may call me a prince

But I'm no such thing
I'm regal, I'm mighty, I'm crowned, I'm king

For those who wonder
We are all kings and queens in our own minds and worlds
It's up to you to embrace it and live the life you've been dreaming
And I will wear my crown with pride
Because I bow to no one

CH. 29: Believe

Sometimes all it takes for someone to believe in themselves is for someone to believe in them. We have all experienced things that may have broken us, or caused wounds that last a lifetime but there is an immense beauty in brokenness. The fact that many of us are still standing is a representation of our ability to survive the worst of times and to withstand future obstacles. A lot of people wonder "why me". Maybe you were picked because you were the one who was best able to handle circumstances that if given to someone else, they might not have survived. What makes me unique is my ability to break and heal, and rise in every step of the process.

What makes us strong is our ability to navigate our obstacles. Many of us have had bad days, and most of us have survived them. Being able to endure a storm that knocks down many things around you, demonstrates your value. Because of my ability to survive adversity, I am able to believe in myself. Some people may see you as damaged goods, but those are the ones that are priceless. We do not come at a cost like most do because our expense cannot be calculated. We may have faced many things, but we have not fallen to anything. Most people who judge based on the damages you've inherited would fold in the same circumstance that caused you to have a bruise. This is why it is imperative that we hold on to hope and faith despite what circumstances we may encounter.

Believe

Encouraging with words of wisdom
Through your tough times
I present you with a rhythm
To find a path within this rhyme
And if it be only one line
One line that reaches your mind
Then my purpose has been touched
To make a believer believe through time

A broken heart is one that could be healed
A wet tear is one that could be dried
A dark night is one that could be lit
A lost key is one that could be found
Believe in yourself

A broke heart is one that could be priceless
An emotionless mind is one that could cry
A slow progression is one that is
Believe in brokenness

I believe in those who don't believe
Because I can be the hope
And leave the hopeless
So that the home doesn't turn into the hopeless whose hope lost
Because they hoped less

I believe in those who don't believe
Because I can be the faith
And leave them faithful

So that the faith can remain faithful because I kept the faith full

I believe in those who don't believe
Because I can be the peace
And leave them peaceful
So that the peace doesn't become peace-less because they lost pieces

I believe in
You
Yourself
Your will
And your brokenness
Because
You've endured
You've lost
You've loved
And you've stood
You were the tree with the deepest roots in a windy city
Because in the midst of chaos
You stood strong

You've turned your troubles into triumphs
Your cats into lions
Your insanes into asylums
Your enemies to alliance

You were flawed and favored
Struggle and success
Ripped and tailored
Broken but blessed

Surviving 100% of your worst days
Your struggle built strength
Don't build a house on a broken foundation
And your life with be length

Believe
In yourself
Because there is a road to escape
No loose brick will cause your downfall

If you believe

CH. 30: The Sun

I am surrounded by a lot of Negative Nancy's, so it is my responsibility to be a Positive Patty in my life. I was surrounded by people who bet that I would falter. These people did not believe in me, and tried to persuade me to give up. They tried to convince me that giving up would be easier because then I would be able to move on and stop wasting time. Although they were saying these types of things to me, I knew what I wanted and I was facing exactly what I needed to in order to get to my destination. These were people who saw the rain and storms in my life that did not realize that at the end of every storm there is a rainbow.

Maya Angelou was the person that shed this type of light into my life. As I was dwelling on the storms, I heard her sing a melody that went *"when it looked like the sun wouldn't shine anymore, God put a rainbow in the clouds".* The rainbow represents the end of a storm; it's a signal of hope that says you've survived. Many people want the rainbows in life without having to go through the storm. The sun may not be there before, after, or during the storm. Sometimes we seek light that is not present in the moments we need them, but that is when the rainbow comes to assure you that everything is just fine.

I have encountered many instances that made me question whether or not I will be able to withstand this storm. With those instances, there were people that encouraged my thought that I would not be able to survive. However, each time I did not see the light, there was a rainbow that God showed me. Every time this happened, there was a light inside of me that grew brighter and brighter with every storm that passed. Then, there was one time during one bad storm where I almost listened to the people that told me I would not survive. I approached their darkness but as I got closer they slithered away because what I had not realized is that the light inside of me was only blinding to those who did not believe in my ability to overcome until it was time to get up close and personal.

I stood face to face with my enemies who could not harm me because of the light inside of me that was protecting me. No one promised that the sun would shine every day, but when it doesn't, look for that rainbow.

The Sun

I’ve become blinded by this everlasting darkness
Waiting for a spot of light to shine my way
Then this monster, this heathen, this snake, this lockness
Said, “Oh, that sun won’t shine today”

So, I sang *“when it looked like the sun wouldn’t shine anymore,*
God put a rainbow in the clouds”

When I lost the seed, I planned to grow inside the woman
I cried out with all my grief and no one heard me but Jesus
A couple of forever’s is what we were supposed to be
But the moon, the sun, didn’t shine on me

Then the small waves became tsunami’s
The gray skies grew black
The snake slithered up
And said “That sun won’t be back”

So, I sang *“when it looked like the sun wouldn’t shine anymore,*
God put a rainbow in the clouds.”

But then the light turned dark
And the darkness whispered “come to me”
“Come to me, I won’t bite”
So I went into the darkness that seemed friendly
But then as I stepped closer, the smiles turned to frowns
And the darkness backed down
There was a light inside of me that only I could see
Even though it was dark and cloudy,

There was something inside of me that lit bright
Then I thought that someone is protecting me
I am protected
I am shielded by a higher power
I am guarded by the almighty
Even when the sun won't shine

So, I sang *"when it looked like the sun wouldn't shine anymore,*
God put a rainbow in the clouds."

When a heathen tried to steal my joy
God put a rainbow in the clouds
When the snakes tried to slither into my life
God put a rainbow in the clouds
When the monster tried to break me down
God put a rainbow in the clouds
And when the lockness tried to diminish my message
God put a rainbow in the clouds

I don't need the sun because I have a light inside of me that shines bright
When they thought I was going to fall in the darkness
I walked by faith and not by sight
When they tried to steal my light
I didn't have to fight
Because my might
My power
My confidence
And my height
Protected me from the darkness
Even when the sun didn't shine
And when I lit bright

I watched them scatter back into the darkness
Then I looked up and saw the cloudy day
And realized there was a rainbow in the clouds

And so, I sang *"when it looked like the sun wouldn't shine anymore,*
God put a rainbow in the clouds."

CH. 31: The Crown ain't Worth Much

Don't spend so much time trying to obtain the crown that you forget about the person who it is meant for (yourself). It may look regal, but a crown can make even a peasant look the part even though deep down they will never be as such. It's too heavy for the light-headed because only strong minds, who stood the test, can withstand the weight that comes with wearing a crown. The crown isn't worth much as long as the person wearing it is worth more. The crown is just a compliment of the person wearing it; it does not make the person, the person makes it.

I can bend the crown, step on it, and put it through a tree shredder and it will not make me any less of a king then I already am. But beware of the person who scrambles when their crown is destroyed because that would mean that the extent of their power lies with the crown and not themselves. The crown only hurts to wear when it is not meant for the person for which it is worn. For these people, the crown is worth a lot; however, for the people whose value isn't defined by materialistic things, it's not worth much.

The Crown ain't Worth Much

This crown that I wear is jewelled with many stones
The many stones that people threw at me
Everyone wants a crown but is it worth it?
Was it worth it?
Piece by piece is how this crown came together
Yea it may look nice but how does it feel?
I can tell you it's heavy
It makes it hard to keep your head up
It adds weight to your shoulders
It leaves a ring around your head that forms a crease
But no need to worry about that because it hides that slight imperfection
It's seen as a trophy
It's felt like a prize
It tastes like victory
But its shine blinds your eyes

The Crown ain't worth much

It's a package deal that comes with rebels and peasants
Fame and riches
Glitz and glamor
But pain and stitches
Not everyone can wear it because it hurts
A lot of people don't have what it takes to wear a crown
The journey along the way is a rough one
And the reward at the end is sweet
It has more carats than bugs bunny
But you must be broke, tired, and beat
To get to it

The Crown ain't worth much

Some people train to wear the crown
But the crown is wearing them
Whether its bronze, silver or gold
It doesn't matter if it fits
We do things for things
Instead of doing things for us
And now those things that we get
Are the things that define us
Until it rusts

The Crown ain't worth much

If you sell souls for the crown
The crown is wearing you
If you fight for the crown
Then the crown just beat you
The crown is not the reward
But the feeling is
It's going to cost you bridges, promise rings, and daps
Your sanity, your peace, and your clout
But is it worth it?

The Crown ain't worth much

It may be heavy
It may be uncomfortable
It may weigh you down
But that comes with the territory
If the crown wears you

But if it fits just right

Makes you much stronger
If it keeps you on your feet
Then we wear the crown
But the crown isn’t worth much when the journey is worth more
The crown isn’t worth much when your sanity costs more
So, you keep your crown filled with peasants’ stones and rebels’ rocks
Because this crown ain't worth much
Because I am worth more

Phase 5:

The In-between

CH. 32: Dream

Martin Luther King's "I Have a Dream" speech still holds true till this day. Unfortunately, the reality is that this was the dream that kept on dreaming. It is hard to have a unified United States when its foundation is filled with division. The truth is that we have never been unified, and the only progression we've made is the superior race telling the inferior that "we can be in the same restaurant now". The only progress that we've made (if you should call it that) is that there is no more segregation, but the beliefs behind it still hold true. In fact, maybe we've taken further steps behind because not only is it African Americans, but many other minorities as well like Asians and Mexicans. Unfortunately, speaking about racism at this point in time has succumbed to the ideology of beating a dead horse. Now, people loathe when you pull the race card because they have heard it all before and quite frankly, they are tired of hearing it. But people are tired of experiencing it and having to inform people that what they say or maybe do is prejudice just because they grew up in a household where those behaviors are taught or reinforced.

It makes me think what it means to be a citizen of the United States of America. It means that African Americans don't have to be a slave no more, but systems are put into place so that idea of slavery holds true to some degree. It means that if you were not here when America was first built even though the land was stolen, then you should stay on your side of the border because they don't need criminals corrupting the system even more. It means that Native Americans from whom this land was stolen from murderers, rapists and criminals, get the finders/keepers treatment even though it was theirs to begin with. It means that Asians are oftentimes the invisible/unacknowledged race, until it comes to diseases like COVID 19. It means that Muslim's and Middle Eastern People are the most feared because there may be terrorists among them. Wow, there's a lot to unpack here. It's almost like as time progresses more prejudices and racism is developed and reinforced. I would like for America to be truly unified in all shades, but that's the dream that somehow keeps on dreaming.

Dream

I have a dream that one day this nation will rise up and live out the true meaning of its creed

I have a dream that one day on the red hills of Georgia, the sons of former slaves and the sons of former slave owners will be able to sit down together at the table of brotherhood

I have a dream that one day even the state of Mississippi, a state sweltering with the heat of injustice, sweltering with the heat of oppression, will be transformed into an oasis of freedom and justice

I have a dream that my four little children will one day live in a nation where they will not be judged by the color of the skin but by the content of their character

I have a dream today that one day down in Alabama with its vicious racist, with its governor having his lips dripping with the words of interposition and nullification

One day right there in Alabama little black boys and black girls will be able to join hands with little white boys and white girls with sisters and brothers

I have a dream today!!

I have a dream
The storm will eventually run out of rain
The whips won't be disguised as chains
The ropes won't be disguised as bullets

I have a dream
That peace doesn't have to come with death
That all lives really mean all lives
And that this new slave era will bring a new dawn

I have a dream
That these dreams will come true
That this poem will have a happy ending
That unity will rise over the horizon in all shades

I have a dream
That is just a dream

CH. 33: One Day

We long for the day when we are able to say we've made it. We long for the day when we have the same tears, but better circumstances. We long for the day when we are able to see the results of being crushed so much. We are like grapes being turned into wine. I know that me being crushed like this is for a reason that causes me to be better, more valuable, and more prosperous than ever before. We undergo the most pressure because we have to be made into something worth dying for.

We are all waiting for that one day when we can say it was all worth it. Although we may not be credited for what we have been through, our scars will show what we have survived and we do not need acknowledgment to know our value because it speaks for itself.

This is something that I had to constantly remind myself while facing adversity. This growth mindset is what kept me moving forward. There were many times that I expected that I was not going to make it through because of what circumstances looked like, but oftentimes we are not our expectations. I truly believe that the anxiety and depression that we have developed in this seemingly traumatic process will be well worth it one day.

One Day

One day something will give
I don't know when
But one day
I'll be so full of life
That no heart attack will make me empty
Hopefully,
One day

One day these tears will be dry
This dry will be joy
The joy will be faith
And this faith will not fold

One day all these tears I cry for worry
Will be for peace
One day these screams I shout for brokenness
Will be for healing
One day this pain I feel for scars
Will be for thriving
Hopefully,
One day

One day the doors they close
Will be open
One day these locks they set
Will be cracked
One day the discredit they give
Will be credited
One day these falls I make
Will be risen
One day this black we wear
Will be for wealth not profit

Weight not baggage
Strength not weakness
Healed not beaten
Stood not seated
Saved not deleted
Scared but treated
Hopefully,
One day

The no's will be yes
My goals will progress
My holes will suppress
My fate will finesse
And this mask will undress
One day

My heart will be healed
My soul will be revealed
My fate will be sealed
And my card will be reeled
One day

This stomach that turns will burn with butterflies I earned
Because I stood firm when it was me that they churned
But I learned that life can be healthy with knots
Or fall apart when permed
One day

The shot you shoot will lift your soul
The nights we're down
The roses underground
The smiles turned frowns
The chips turned pounds

Upon your shoulders
Shall seal every crack in your heart
And provide a way for every path that you walk
Hoping
For that one day to come

We will all be free
From this mental cell where WE
Hold the key
One day
That day will come

CH. 34: Love

Although I love many people, I have never been in love. I am not one who knows how to love someone because I have never done it. I've learned to shield my heart from people in order to make heartbreak less likely. I had come to a point in my life that I tend to distance myself from people who I feel I am developing a connection with. I have been hurt a lot, so I do this to prevent myself from being hurt more. I am one who believes that the more people you have in your life, the more problems. Quite frankly, I don't have time for any more problems to resurface in my life because I wanted to make the foolish decision to develop a connection with someone. In life, I have grown to become comfortable with being alone rather than rely on people just so they can disappoint. It took a while to get to this point, and some would call the journey horrific.

In the beginning, I had to learn how to develop a healthy way to love, but had no idea how to do that. That was until I realized that in order to have a true meaningful love for other people, you have to know how to love yourself first. Learning to appreciate myself and grow comfortable with being me unapologetically was difficult. I learned that I had to give at least the same amount of love that I give to other people to myself. Once I was able to do that, it became easier to navigate my way through relationships. By relationships, I mean social interactions with friends and acquaintances. I know how to not love too deeply because the depth of your love today can be the depth of your wound tomorrow.

Some may call this unorthodox, but I love myself so much that if it were just me on this earth, I'd be extremely happy. But just to clarify, this is not because I despise the human race necessarily, it's just that I have a preference. And that preference is me, myself, and I. I smile from ear to ear knowing that if I were going through something difficult, I can count on myself to guide me through.

This love that I have for myself was not always present. I did not meet people's expectations of love, nor did I care to. I never said I was going to meet your expectations nor did I know what they were. Acting with assumptions can be a very dangerous game. I am at a point in life where if someone feels a slight uncomfortability with me, the door will always be open for you to exit. Hell, I may even kick you out of it to minimize the risk of you corrupting my personal space. Now, I know how to have relationships, but I know to not expect anything from them. A lot of people I encounter are peasants anyways so in that sense, it is much easier to say "adios muchachos" or "bye Felicia".

In other news, this next poem was written during a period where my mind struggled to find a place where I can build or grow a new love for myself after being in a place where depression lived for so long.

Love

How can I love you if I cannot love myself
I have learned to pick the black rose in a field of red ones
Dead trees stand tall outside my house
With a sign on it that reads "love don't live here"

This is because my home remains lifeless
The broken shutters
The faded bricks
The boarded windows

Love don't live here

It's better off torn down because I don't have the skill level to build up
I could buy a new one, but I don't have that type of money
I used it all on this one
And now I own damaged products

I have a nice house
But my home is damaged
Love don't live here
So how can I love you if I cannot love myself

CH. 35: Looking Back

To dwell on the past means that you have not healed from what caused you to have hurt. Every time I would look back into the past, I would have grief from what I experienced. It truly hurt to look back at the lows and the situations that caused me to break. I was in the present living in the past and ignoring the future. The past is meant to be lessons learned so you can ensure that you do not make the same mistakes in the future or in the present.

Moving on can be very difficult when holding on to hurt because the weight of it slows you down. Some people say pick up the pieces and keep going; however, I say let it be what it was, leave the pieces, and learn from it. Oftentimes, when we carry these pieces throughout life, you are carrying small bits of that pain that makes it difficult to function.

I was unable to function because I focused so much on what has happened to me rather than where I go from here. However, it is important to note that ignoring your past traumas will only cause them to resurface at a greater extent later on in life. We shouldn't bottle our feelings up to deal with later. I found it better to deal with what is causing you to be in disarray in the moment it is occurring, then to move on from that moment. We should not make moments last a lifetime which is why a dwell on the past is a bruise for the future.

Looking Back

Looking back
I would have cried
I would have went
I would have sighed
Looking back
I would have tried
To get some closure beyond my cries

Looking back
Letting go
Of my own blood
Of my own lows
Looking back
I would be high
If I had went,
If I had cried

Looking back
If I could see
The very hurt
Beneath my grief
Looking back
If I could see
My blind would brail
My mind would be free

Looking back
I'm looking back
I'm in the past
I see my cracks
Looking back

I wouldn't have looked
Because what I saw
It made me shook
I'm looking back

CH. 36: Poetry

For me, poetry was a place where I could be truly free. It was my great escape where I could express the pains crying from the depths of my soul and feel like I just released a thousand pounds. Through poetry, I was able to express all my hurt, pain, and prosperity without providing specific details of each instance. I could write any and everything that the general public might not understand otherwise, or won't accept. I can be care-free and touch other people's emotions without actually saying a peep. It is a superpower that I am able to use to freely touch or even control the minds that are willing to listen. It is something that provides me the opportunity to be the narrator of hundreds of lives. Poetry is a place where I can say what I mean, and hide it so that no one knows exactly where my mind is. It is a place where I can hide the smallest voice behind the loudest scream.

Poetry is something that gives people the opportunity to have their own unique meanings with just one line. Poetry is something that I used to heal all wounds including many others. It is something where I can truly say God is poetry in which I can choose to be the creator. Poetry creates power and influence, and costs me nothing to make. Poetry is a place where I can be flat-broke and feel like the richest man in the world.

Poetry is limitless. Poetry gives me a power that is unmatched by any of the most powerful people on earth. It gives me the power to break, crumble, build, heal, and even give voices to the silence. Poetry is a medicine that no doctor can prescribe.

To step into the true power of poetry, you have to have the ability to make people feel using your voice both on and off the paper. In that sense, I am a unique poet. I am able to step into my power because I realize that there is not only volume in the things you say, but also how you say it. My poetry does not just come from my mind; it comes from my mind, body, and soul. My true power shows when all three are in harmony.

Physical beings die all the time, but poetry lasts a lifetime. Poetry is a place where I can live on forever beyond my years on this earth. Poetry is only hard to comprehend for people who are closed-minded. To understand what a poem is truly meant to do, you must eliminate the idea of assumptions and open your heart to be touched by someone you may not trust but know wouldn't cause any damage. This final chapter, if the rest of the book has not already, is meant to help you open a chamber of your mind that may not have been tapped into before this moment.

Poetry

A coded language
A daring try to write all the things you cannot say
A game to play with people's emotion
Where for one moment,
The birth of a poem is a result of freedom of the mind
and a union between your mind, body, and soul

A place where no one can find you
Where poetic lines can be read however your mind wants to
Where the depressed go to cry
Where the heart-broken go to heal
Where the ugly feels beautiful
Literatures most legendary and important component
Poetry

Is something that appears when your mind takes a vacation
Poetry is the God of all senses
For when it's called upon it feels like Jesus lost control of the world
It can give you invincibility and courage
Empathy and anger
Motivation and inspiration
Life and death

But to be poetic
Is to be fearless
To be poetic
Is to have might
To be poetic
Is to have the ability to change minds
To be poetic
Is to have power and control

And to be poetic
Is to believe your life is poem

Poetry
Where I can say the same thing twice and have a different meaning each time
Where I can say whatever the hell I want because there are no penalties
Where I have the power to break and heal at the same time
A priceless medicine

Where people can hear your story without hearing your story
It is meant to be felt
Poetry is something where death can't do us part
It's everlasting
It is something that surfaces where one experiences something that opens their mind
Something the closed-minded cannot comprehend
Lying deep between these lines
Poetry

Epilogue

The essence of an ill mind shall not lean on your own understanding. Poetry and telling my story were a healing for me. It took me a while to realize that the sick mind that got me here, will not be the mind that will get me out of here. My point is that there is a power in words that changes the course of a life. Everyone has circumstances that make people do the craziest of things, and sometimes there is nothing you can do to change that. However, people hold the ability to change themselves if they learn how to navigate their ill mind to their benefit.

When life goes crumbling, the process has begun where different phases in your life will become prominent in teaching you how to move forward. Obstacles are nothing but a blessing in disguise. Every breaking moment is an opportunity for a new beginning. It's the urge to give up during phase 2 of this life-long process that is hard to resist. However, it was in these moments where I made a vow to myself that everywhere I go, I am going to let my light shine. One of my inspirations, Maya Angelou, says that there are always illuminations above the sky, but the clouds cover them, so we cannot see them, but when there is an illumination in the clouds, there is a message of hope that is imparted upon your mind that the storm has passed. We must remember that we are a product of our ancestors who chose to survive.

I am a survivor of depression and much more because I made a conscious decision, with an ill mind, to survive when I felt the want not to. This means that I was not accepting of my current self, circumstances, or anything else that had to do with Julius Gibbs. I did not know how to be him, nor did I like his circumstances, so I tried everything I could to get rid of him. I used to want to be a chef, I used to want to be a musician, I used to want to be a soldier, but before I could do any of that, I had to learn how to be myself. That was the challenge. I was not the person who received the best grades in college, was an athlete, a physical stud, or any of the sorts. In fact, people told me that you do not seem like the military type. So, what made me special? What made me unique? I realized that what made me unique is that I was not the cookie cutter student who "drank the Kool-aid". I was a proud member of the rock bottom association. But you want to know what made me unique that separated me from everyone else? What if I told you I "got by" with my circumstances of functional abdominal pain, IBS, depression and suicidal ideations, precancerous lesions, and numerous other things that hindered my ability to perform. My mere presence alone speaks volumes of my strength. What if I told you that during this time, I wrote and published two books and working on the third, became an SEO of a website where I publish poetry, created a forum for people who struggle with depression, and saved 6 people from committing suicide whom was in the midst of the act? I may look like I didn't challenge myself, but I am able to succeed saying that I've become an author, poet, entrepreneur, activist, and survivor in the process which makes me unique. And the funny part is, it was the essence of an ill mind that got me into this position.

I had a follower who tried to hang himself from a bed post because he was struggling with depression, and all the negative words and thoughts had projected him too far. I had a follower who reached out saying he wanted to slit his wrists because he didn't feel like his life was progressing and wasn't getting acceptance or recognition from other people. He felt he was not good enough. I know of a young man who pops pills, almost fist-full sometimes, frequently because he tries to numb himself from his life circumstances that fell out of his control. I know of a person who was battling with his identity and was ridiculed so much that he sat at the top of a rooftop wondering if there was any other choice. I know of a man who shot himself in the head to silence his thoughts because they screamed that he wasn't going anywhere in life and that this was it. I know of a girl who's very talented but gives up because of her self-image and lack of confidence and is afraid of what other people will think. My point is that when was the last time you spoke life or hope into someone else and picked them up in the midst of their discouragement. When was the last time someone spoke hope into you? People will label you by your faults, your weaknesses, and your insecurities. Oftentimes, when we point out what's wrong with someone else, we don't have to look at what's wrong with ourselves. Learn to walk in your worth. You can decide that life isn't worth living but how would you know? You've never picked up the battle nor fought in it. You were faced with something that you thought you couldn't handle and decided it wasn't worth it. But when will it be worth it? If you don't like this world, make it a better one.

I am what happens when God says yes. I had been falsely accused, ridiculed, dismissed, and disregarded. I've lost friendships, my character was diminished, I had raging anxiety, and depression. I was truly crumbling but still God said yes. There is immense beauty in your brokenness when God says yes. Because he said yes, I walk in faith, and not by sight every day of my life. I rose despite my circumstances. God worked against all odds, he helped me relieve the burden on my shoulders, and removed all things that would work against his power so that I can have a testimony. All the things

I had been through told me many stories of why I would not prosper. But when God said yes, he said no weapon formed against me shall prosper; he said having stood the test I shall receive the crown of life, and that we are not broken beyond repair. In these times, he sent an Angel who whispered in my ear "we shall face many defeats, but we shall not be defeated."

So, when life goes crumbling, resist the urge to give up and resist the urge to quit because there is an illumination waiting to appear from your cloud in the moment when life goes crumbling. And as Maya Angelou would say, "We may encounter many defeats, but we shall not be defeated."

www.ingramcontent.com/pod-product-compliance
Lightning Source LLC
LaVergne TN
LVHW090947080826
845145LV00003B/926

* 9 7 8 0 5 7 8 9 0 5 4 8 8 *